THE BEGINNER'S GUIDE TO
Landscape Painting

THE BEGINNER'S GUIDE TO
Landscape Painting

Kimm Stevens

MAGNA BOOKS

Published by Magna Books
Magna Road
Wigston
Leicester LE18 4ZH

Produced by Bison Books Ltd
Kimbolton House
117A Fulham Road
London SW3 6RL

ISBN 1-85422-625-8

Printed in Hong Kong

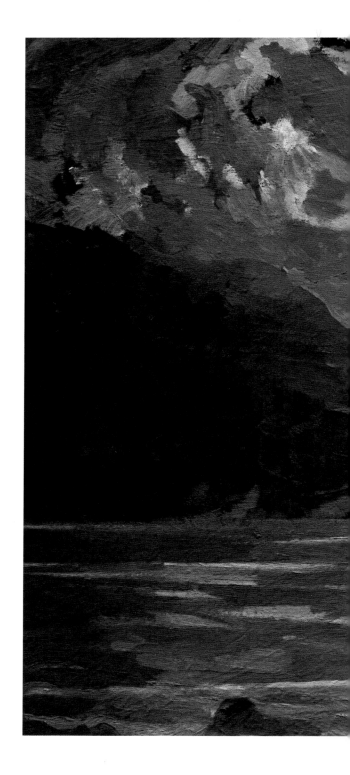

PAGE 1
Peter Lloyd-Jones
Coombe Lake
Oil, 14 × 14 inches (35.8 × 35.8 cm)

PAGE 2-3
Kimm Stevens
Esher Common
Pastel, 21 × 30 inches (54 × 72 cm)

RIGHT
Kimm Stevens
Ullswater
Oil on canvas, 25 × 41 inches (64 × 105 cm)

Contents

1. History

For centuries artists have been preoccupied with the desire to depict their surroundings. The images which they create inevitably derive from their immediate experience; whatever requirements their culture places upon them, be it the church, the state or the wealthy, they respond with imagery derived from their own experience and surroundings. This immediate response to nature brings an originality and freshness to painting which is common to all cultures, whether the image is an Egyptian tomb painting of a pond filled with fish and surrounded by ibis; a view of a fourteenth-century Flemish town glimpsed through a nativity scene; or a busy nineteenth-century Parisian street scene.

This spark of originality, the freshness of realism taken directly from nature, draws on common ground from generation to generation, and talks across the centuries far more effectively than the themes which the paintings are intended to depict. It is a fundamental justification for the existence and practice of landscape painting. Nature, animals, landscape and the human figure are common to all cultures.

The first true landscape – that is, a painting depicting nothing but landscape – appeared in seventeenth-century Holland. Prior to this, landscape was used as a background to the narration of a classical, mythological or religious story. In Botticelli's *La Primavera*, Flora strides out of an enchanted wood, flowers pouring from her mouth, bedecking the land with Spring. In Titian's fabulous *Bacchus and Ariadne* (pages 8-9), the reveling Bacchantae crash through the trees to meet Ariadne, who is looking out across a great sweeping coastline at her fleeing lover's boat disappearing over the horizon. In Campin's *Virgin and Child before a Fire Screen* (right), we see through the window an exquisite urban landscape of people going about their daily life.

By the seventeenth century, the landscape was beginning to dominate the painting and the subject and action became less significant. In Claude's *Landscape with Psyche outside the Palace of Cupid*, the figure of

Psyche is dwarfed by the magnificence and enchantment of the landscape while in *Seaport and the Embarkation of Saint Ursula* the human drama is overshadowed by the superb light and atmosphere. Artists were using their painting of classical events as a vehicle to portray the more fundamental and expressive realism that nature and landscape offered.

RIGHT
Robert Campin
Virgin and Child before a Firescreen, c.1430
Oil on wood, 25 × 19¼ inches (63.5 × 49.5 cm)
This domestic Flemish Nativity has a wonderful example of contemporary fourteenth-century urban life depicted through the window (detail below).

In the more puritanical and commercially-oriented society of seventeenth-century Holland, the concept of realism was accepted as a viable end in itself. The re-formed church was strongly opposed to any iconography and the merchant classes wanted to celebrate power through wealth, both in property and land. It is in the seventeenth century, therefore, that landscape painting emerges as an individual genre: in France with the classical paintings of Poussin and Claude Lorraine; in Holland with the paintings of Ruysdael, Cuyp and Hobbema; and in Belgium, slightly earlier, with a small number of stunning paintings by Rubens. It was in Holland that artists began to paint the landscape as it was, deriving both composition and harmony directly from nature, with no allusion to the classical or mythological. In Hobbema's *The Avenue, Middelharnis* (pages 12-13), the use of direct observation and the geometrical harmony of the composition are as effective now, 300 years later, as they were at the time.

Rubens and his studio produced a staggering number of massively powerful Baroque paintings, but throughout his life he also painted portraits and paintings on a more personal level, to commemorate events in his life. One example is *Autumn Landscape with a View of Het Steen in the Early Morning* (page 14), his magnificent house and the land surrounding it bathed in early morning sunlight. The painting celebrates both Rubens' land and his life, and he takes great pleasure in detailing minutely the landscape he knows, but it is also a celebration of the magnificence of nature, the great sweeping vista, the blazing sunrise in a vaulting, cloud-filled sky.

By the eighteenth century the focus of landscape painting had moved across the Channel to Britain, where two main strands of topographical and romantic painting developed. Britain, geographically on the perimeter of European culture, had by then emerged as a major commercial, industrial and colonial power and was spreading her influence throughout the world. It was natural, therefore, that the educated and the aristocratic should make it an essential part of their education to embark on the Grand Tour of Europe, visiting the major cities and assimilating the modern and ancient artifacts of Italy and Greece. The cultural identity of Britain was enhanced by the return of these travelers, bringing with them work by artists such as Caneletto and Guardi, as well as Greek and Roman works.

RIGHT
Titian
Bacchus and Ariadne, 1522-23
Oil on canvas, 69 × 75 inches (173 × 191 cm)
This painting, with its theme of classical mythology, was executed as part of a series of paintings to decorate a room in the palace of Alfonso d'Este, at Ferrara, the others being painted by Giorgione and Giovanni Bellini. It is interesting that the decorative figures are rather frieze-like in appearance, flattened and rhythmic, while the landscape plays an enormous part in the painting, the clouds, trees, sky and sea all creating pattern. The space of the landscape is fully developed in its natural form, receding some considerable distance to the horizon.

OVERLEAF
Claude Lorraine
Landscape with Psyche outside the Palace of Cupid, 1664
Oil on canvas, 34¼ × 59½ inches (87 × 151 cm)
Unlike Titian's *Bacchus and Ariadne*, the mythological theme of this painting seems to be much less important than the romantic landscape, which is no mere backdrop to drama, but rather the main subject in which the drama unfolds. It is only a small step from here to painting a landscape for its own merits, rather than as a vehicle for some higher purpose.

Meyndert Hobbema
The Avenue, Middelharnis,
1689
Oil on canvas, 40¾ × 55½
inches (104 × 141 cm)
One of the earliest pure
landscapes, depicting
everyday life in Holland,
this painting is dominated
by the pronounced single-
viewpoint perspective,
which creates a powerful
diagonal cross, forming the
basis of the composition.

The grand tourists also recorded their experiences by using the light and convenient method of watercolor, rather as we would use the camera today. This provided Britain with a rich basis from which the tradition of both topographical and romantic landscape painting emerged. Interestingly, naval officers were also trained in the use of watercolor so that they could record the topography of the New World, which was being opened up to trade and conquest. Of the two strands of landscape painting, objective topographical studies, freshly painted in watercolor, found maturity in the Norwich School with the work of John Sell Cotman and Paul Sandby; the more romantic, dramatic approach was represented by artists such as Richard Wilson, who applied the Italianate classical style of Lorraine and Poussin to the rugged landscapes of the Lake District and Wales.

The two traditions of Grand Tour watercolors and romantic landscape combined and erupted in an explosion of creative genius with the work of Joseph William Mallord Turner (1775-1851). Turner, a great traveler throughout Europe, recorded his journeys in a mass of watercolors and sketchbooks, producing endless studies of light, atmospheric effects, landscapes and seascapes. He captured and exploited the drama of sunlight through direct observa-tion and experience, which he combined with a romantic appreciation of the power and excitement of the natural elements. His work acts as a pivot in landscape painting between the eighteenth-century classicizing tradition following Lorraine, and the more romantic and realist painters that follow.

The other great protagonist of British landscape painting during this period was John Constable. He is in some ways an even more revolutionary and influential painter; his achievement was to observe and record, without pretension or posturing, the Suffolk landscape in which he was brought up. He took the rich cacophony of rain and wind, clouds and trees, and people about their daily work on the River Stour, and held them in a harmonious and deceptively natural composition, painted with an economy that is nonetheless vibrant in detail and incident. Both his modest realism and his novel painting technique, rendering form and space with direct, positive brush strokes of paint, and fragmenting and fracturing images into color and light, was to have a major influence on the development of landscape painting later in the nineteenth century.

At much the same time that Constable was rendering his love of the Suffolk countryside into paint, a group of painters in post-revolutionary France were developing their own form of realism, a realism infused with political idealism for the future rather than poetic yearnings for the past. Millet's *Gleaners* (pages 16-17), a fabulous glowing painting of evening light, shows us the poorest members of the agricultural community scrabbling in the stubble for the last morsels of the harvest while, in the distance, the more prosperous take the year's bounty home. Both Corot and Boudin painted outdoors like Constable but, unlike him, they recognized the value of these *'plein-air'* paintings and were prepared to exhibit them, whereas Constable would work up a studio composition for exhibition.

Plein-air painting, made more convenient by the growing availability of ready-prepared paints in tubes, enabled painters to record nature and the effects of light more swiftly and accurately, and with a more immediate and spontaneous realism. This development led to Impressionism, perhaps the most revolutionary movement in art since the Renaissance, which focused above all on landscape painting and took the realistic depiction of nature as its main subject.

The Impressionists were the first group of artists successfully to suggest that minor everyday events were adequate subjects in

themselves. They did not use their paintings as vehicles for moral or political judgments but painted the world as they saw it. They used new ideas of color and light to show space and form, depicting the world not as the Academies had taught people to see it, but as the individual eye observed it. Color was to be the revolutionary development in Impressionism; hitherto, tone and color had played an important but secondary role in the establishment of space and form. With

ABOVE
John Constable
Stonehenge, 1835
Watercolor
This watercolor combines the vigor and freshness of observed nature with a clear sense of composition and geometry, producing a painting which is naturalistic, yet loaded with romantic import.

Jean-Francois Millet
The Gleaners
Oil on canvas, 32½ × 43¼
inches (83.5 × 111cm)
The drama of light and
color still exists in this
landscape, but the romantic
ideals that are present in
Rubens, Constable and
Turner are tempered with
the harsher realism of
poverty, represented by the
women gleaning the last of
the harvest for their
survival.

the growing understanding of the scientific basis of light, and the increased range of colors available as an offshoot of the chemical and dyeing industries, color became the principal tool for expressing space and light.

The Impressionists, while embracing the full range of subject matter, recognized landscape painting as the key to exploring the possibilities and harmonies of color and form. They exploited the recently discovered fact that color was not inherent in an object, but the result of the way light was reflected from it, and thus subject to constant change and modification. At first the movement was mocked; one critic wrote in 1876: 'Someone should tell M Pissarro forcibly that trees are never violet, that the sky is never the color of fresh butter . . . ' In Monet's deceptively simple painting *Regatta at Argenteuil*, we are presented with bold slashes of blue, orange and white paint, which combine to create a dazzling effect of water while maintaining the individual qualities of the colors. We are as aware of the paint and color as we are of the illusion that they create. This theme runs through all Monet's landscape work and manifests itself

in its full glory through his series of *Haystack* paintings and the superb compositions of waterlilies that he made at the end of his long life.

In Pissarro's *The Côte des Boeufs at L'Hermitage near Pointoise* (overleaf), the very dense and enclosed space of woodland thicket is established through color. The red roofs through the wood complement and break up the greens and browns of the trees so that, once again, what initially appears to be a mass of color suddenly opens up to be a fabulous illusion of space. The sense of being there, and exploring and working out where one is, is extraordinary. The Impressionists succeeded in identifying light and color as crucial in the depiction of their surroundings. Combined with the revolutionary idea that mundane, everyday events and landscapes were valid subjects for serious painting, this laid the foundation for the radical developments that formed the basis for the explosion in creative thinking that has overtaken us in the twentieth century. Landscape, once again, plays an important role in this development.

One painter who worked for a time with

BELOW
Claude Monet
Haystacks, Snow Effect, 1891
Oil on canvas, 25¼ × 36¼ inches (65 × 81 cm)
Like Turner, Monet painted light, but initially in a much more objective, realist manner. He found color in shadows and painted the effects of light with sharp, positive dashes of color. This more direct approach developed in Monet's later years into series of paintings, one being of haystacks, where the observation of light effects on these simple forms takes on such an intensity that they become imbued with a primal power which extends way beyond the objective realism that is at the root of Impressionism.

RIGHT
Frédéric Bazille
Vue de la Village, 1868
Oil on canvas, 51 × 35 inches (130 × 89 cm)
The portrait and the landscape are of equal importance, complementing and reinforcing the realism in this painting.

the Impressionists, Paul Cézanne, felt the need to counteract the inevitable dissolution of form and structure to which painting only in light and color led. He therefore resolved to give greater import and weight to Impressionism by reintroducing rhythm and geometric structure into the fragmented atmospheric color of his contemporaries. Where Monet dissolved form into light dashes of paint, Cézanne reasserted structure by establishing color as a facet of form. In Cézanne's painting, colors not only conveyed space and light but became an integral component of the painting, relating across the surface to one another, so that the painting is not so much an illusion as a harmony of marks that combine to present us with the concrete reality of the subject.

The revolutionary ideas regarding the use of color promulgated by the Impressionists were extended and formulated by Georges Seurat, who recognized the value of fragmented color in breaking up the surface of

the painting to give a sense of light and space. He created the system of painting known as Pointillism, using minute dots of pure color which merged to produce the image. The color he applied was pure and relatively unmixed and his painting achieved an incredible luminosity and brilliance. Like Cézanne, Seurat sought to give compositional order to the atmospheric, spontaneous *plein-air* paintings of the Impressionists. The combined effect of these revolutionary developments was to establish the primacy of form and color over subject matter as the fundamental and critical elements of a painting; landscape, with its ever-changing color, form and space, became a means to explore the possibilities and extremes to which a painting could be taken.

Cézanne had a profound influence on the early twentieth-century painters Braque and Picasso, who interpreted his ordering of space and form as a cue to abandon single-viewpoint perspective and reorganize the

FAR LEFT
Camille Pissarro
The Côte des Boeufs at L'Hermitage, near Pointoise, 1877
Oil on canvas, 45¼ × 34½ inches (115 × 87.6 cm)
The forms of houses and woodland trees emerge from the vibrant juxtaposition of warm and cool colors; the picture unfolds almost entirely through color, in a perfect fusion of paint surface and image.

ABOVE
Georges Seurat
The Canal at Gravelines, 1890
Oil on canvas, 28½ × 36¼ inches (73 × 93 cm)
Seurat extended and developed the color discoveries that the Impressionists made into a more formalized system, in order to achieve maximum luminosity. He applied the paint in small dots of pure color, which merged together in the eye to form the image.

LEFT
Paul Cézanne
Mountains at l'Estaque,
1886-90
Oil on canvas, 21 × 28½
inches (54 × 73 cm)
Impressionist gestures and
delicate renditions of light
and form through color are
formalized and structured
to create these magnificent
compositions by Cézanne.
The structure and form is
not only linear, but extends
through to the use of color,
which is balanced between
red, yellow, green and
blue.

OVERLEAF
André Derain
Collioure, 1905
Oil on canvas, 28 × 35½
inches (72 × 91 cm)
Here form and space are
established almost entirely
through color. At first the
color seems over-
exaggerated, but it is
through this exaggeration
that the full range and
dynamic of color can be
exploited in order to show
space and form in such a
vibrant and exciting way.

canvas to combine multiple viewpoints. The first Cubist paintings, once again, were landscapes, although it must be said that the early Cubists quickly resorted to the more controlable 'landscape' of the still life.

At much the same time, Pointillist painters were using brighter and purer dabs of color, until the younger artists Matisse, Derain and Vlaminck broke out of this potentially stultifying mode and began to paint bold landscapes with the color pitched at its most extreme. Where shadows were subtly cool and blue, they were painted pure bright blue; where the trees were lit by the warm sunlight, they were painted orange and red: this, the Fauve movement, was perhaps the last revolutionary art movement to use landscape objectively. Although the colors were extreme and bright, they followed the fundamental natural harmonies presented by the landscape and were therefore true to the spirit of art following nature. The second generation of Expressionist painters, such as Nolde and Kokoschka, on the other hand, used landscape as a vehicle to express their own deepest feelings.

As the twentieth century progressed, artists became more concerned with personal expression and exploration, and landscape painting became less central to the main stream than it was in the nineteenth century. Nonetheless a considerable number of painters have turned to landscape as a source of inspiration and expression, including the English painters Nash, Sutherland and Piper, with their intensely realized visionary landscapes, and, in the latter years of the twentieth century, Francis Bacon with his desperately sad *Landscapes 1 and 2* and David Hockney's map-like excursions of color trails across California.

In this opening chapter, I have not only tried to describe the course of landscape painting over the past four centuries, but to convey the idea that, for every time and generation, landscape has been used for a different purpose, whether to express power and wealth in the eighteenth century, to charm the nineteenth-century industrialists, or to explore and extend the extremes to which a painting can be taken. Now, as we embark on the twenty-first century, horribly aware of the vulnerability of our environment, landscape as a subject once again becomes relevant: so much so, that artists like Richard Long literally bring great lumps of rock and earth into our galleries to remind us that out there the landscape is wonderful, powerful and full of endless possibilities.

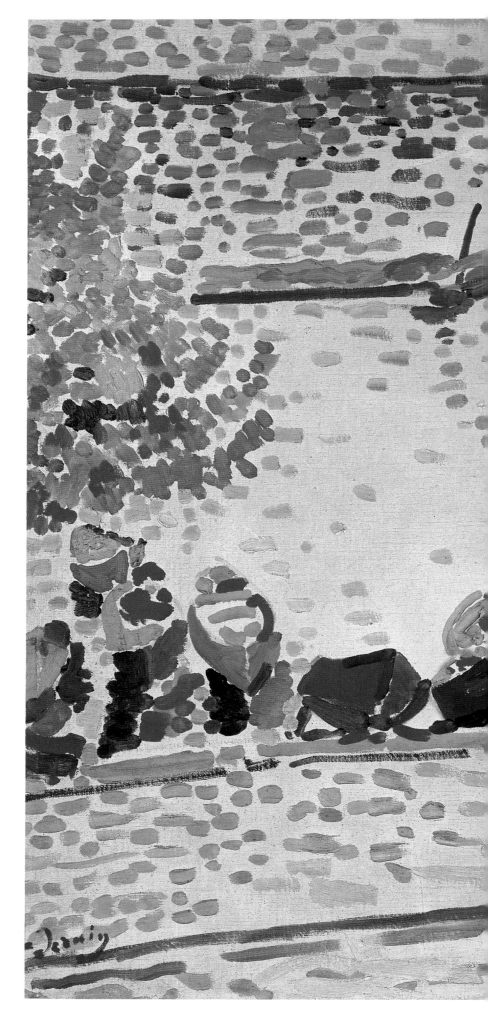

2. Equipment

Basics

When beginning to paint landscape, you need some equipment. This can be extremely rudimentary; I have on occasion been out walking without (dare I say it) any form of drawing equipment, and seen some wonderful effect of light crashing through trees and between buildings. I have had to resort to a ballpoint and the back of an old till receipt out of my pocket – not ideal equipment! – but I have noted down enough to jog my memory about the particular situation and then gone back to get more detailed information. The first things to have if you are interested in the landscape are a small pocket-sized sketchbook, a pen, soft pencil, sharpener and eraser. You should carry these around with you all the time, because you never know when you may see something that you want to paint, and if you are able to make even the briefest of sketches you will remember the idea you had and will be able to elaborate it later.

ABOVE LEFT
Soluble colored pencils combine the advantage of line with the opportunity to paint areas of color and tone. They allow you to make decisive and informative drawings quickly, with the minimum paraphernalia.

LEFT
This pencil sketchbook drawing of a bridge proved very useful as a basis for several studio pastel paintings. By completing a careful measured drawing, one gains considerable understanding of the structure and topography of the view, which helps to sustain more ambitious work away from the subject.

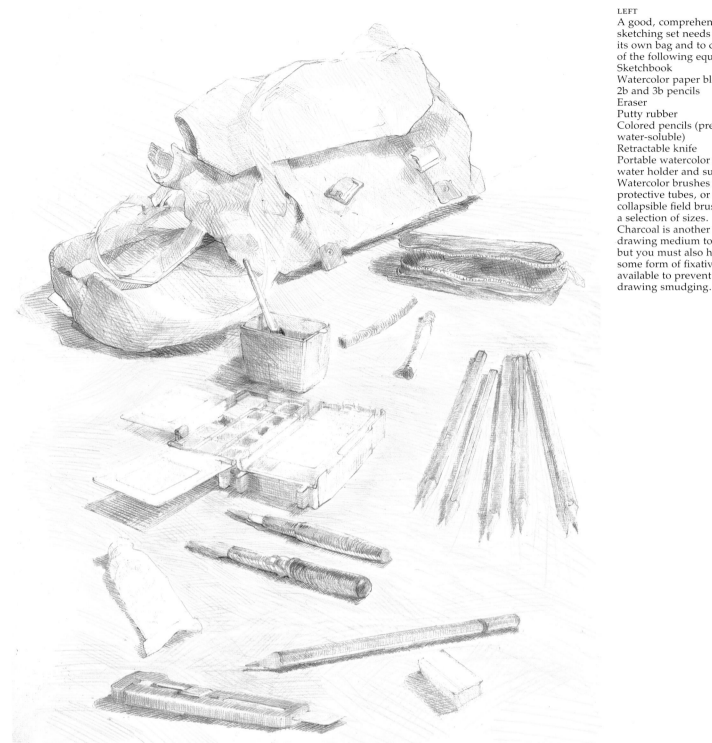

LEFT
A good, comprehensive sketching set needs to have its own bag and to consist of the following equipment:
Sketchbook
Watercolor paper block
2b and 3b pencils
Eraser
Putty rubber
Colored pencils (preferably water-soluble)
Retractable knife
Portable watercolor set with water holder and supply
Watercolor brushes in protective tubes, or collapsible field brushes in a selection of sizes.
Charcoal is another useful drawing medium to carry, but you must also have some form of fixative available to prevent the drawing smudging.

Water-Soluble Pencils

The idea for the painting is the most elusive thing and must be caught on the instant. Pocket-sized equipment can most easily be extended to embrace color by including colored pencils. A small set of ten can be carried discreetly in pocket or bag and gives you much more flexibility and variety in sketching. A further refinement can be to have water-soluble colored pencils, which can be dissolved and brushed out on the paper to make color wash drawings. For this you will need a folding brush, and the paper in your sketch book must be sturdy enough to be made wet. The main problem with water-soluble pencils is that you need a small supply of water to use them, though it is amazing how you can improvise. I hesitate to advocate the use of spit but it does work! A more effective (and hygienic) solution is to carry a small plastic screw-top medicine bottle, either already filled or to be filled on site; water often features in landscapes so you can use the river, pond or lake (or puddle) as a supply.

Watercolors

The next piece of equipment that is extremely useful, and enables you to make complete paintings, is a set of watercolors. Watercolors come either in pans or tubes. The pans need to be kept in a purpose-built box which usually has a built-in palette and space to keep a brush. The tubes can be kept loose, but obviously you will need some kind of palette (see page 32) for mixing your paints. Pans are very convenient and light and are particularly useful for fieldwork because the set is self-contained. Some sets come complete with their own water bottle and container.

Tubes enable you to mix greater quantities of color more quickly for large washes, although they are more bulky to carry. With watercolors you need specific paper, because the technique uses the white of the paper as the source of light and the rough texture to promote richness of color and tone (see page 39). A small block of watercolor paper should therefore be included in the set. It would still be possible to carry all this equipment fairly discreetly in various pockets or a large handbag, but it is becoming sufficiently bulky to warrant a specially designed art bag.

Brushes

For watercolor you will need some sable brushes or good quality synthetic versions; the brush hairs should be springy and bounce back into shape when wet. The hairs

ABOVE
A selection of pages from various sketchbooks is shown above and on pages 29 and 30. Some sketches collect information, or stand on their own, others are a more intuitive response to the landscape and serve as a trigger for the memory. Both approaches are valuable, and both should be pursued.

LEFT
Clova Stuart-Hamilton
Autumn, Rueyres
Watercolor, 4½ × 8 inches (11.5 × 20.5 cm)
This approach to watercolor builds up the picture in small brushstrokes, producing a homogenous image. Each brushstroke is of a pure color, which prevents the watercolor from becoming muddy and maintains a clarity and lightness of touch.

of a round brush, even a large one, should come to a pointed tip. Sable brushes are expensive but will last many years if you clean them regularly and thoroughly. Cheap brushes can prove a false economy.

Round brushes are the most versatile as they can lay in broad washes or produce a delicate line at the tip. Flat brushes produce block-like marks which can be very useful for building up form and bringing washes to sharply defined edges in a crisp and decisive manner. Brushes are very vulnerable and should be kept in a ridged plastic tube to protect the hairs; field brushes retract into the handle when not in use, thus protecting the hairs. These are very useful, although they can occasionally retract while you are painting, which is a little disconcerting!

Watercolor brushes come in different sizes from 000 (very small) right up to 16 (really big). Most beginners instinctively go for smaller brushes, as they seem to offer more control, but the larger the brush the more paint it holds, so you do not have to keep returning to the palette to replenish your brush. If it is a good brush, it will come to a point so that it will be possible to do delicate and intricate work even with a larger

size, so be bold: go for a larger brush size than you think is necessary. Of course, the final choice rests with your own inclinations and approach, and for extremely intricate work, the smaller brushes are essential.

Ginny Chalcraft
La Rague, South of France
Watercolor, 9½ × 13½ inches (24.3 × 34.5 cm)
This painting shows a strong decisive approach to watercolor painting; the artist has placed the paint in well-defined areas of tone and color, which builds up the image across the page. The result is both crisp and controled, enabling the very fluid medium of watercolor to convey a considerable amount of information.

This sketchbook study of a palm tree was a spur-of-the-moment creation.

ABOVE
Sketchbook study.

LEFT
A basic set of oil paints, suitable for field work, should comprise the following:
Paint box
Tubes of the oil colors titanium white, lemon yellow, cadmium yellow, cadmium red, crimson, magenta, ultramarine, cobalt blue and cerulean blue (if you wish to paint with a lower key palette, include venetian red, yellow ocher, burnt sienna, raw umber, burnt umber and terre verte)
Palette
Jar of white/mineral spirit
Double screw-top dipper filled with pure linseed oil and turpentine
Set of bristle brushes sizes 4, 6, 8 and 10, both flat and round
Palette knife
Rags
Sketching easel.

FAR RIGHT
These two charts show a practicable layout of color on the palette, and the colors that offer the most flexibility and range in mixing. The first consists of a version of each saturated primary: white, lemon yellow, cadmium yellow, cadmium red, magenta, ultramarine blue, cobalt blue and cerulean blue. The second is a more subdued and subtle range of earth colors: white, lemon yellow, yellow ocher, venetian red, rose madder, burnt sienna, raw umber, burnt umber, ultramarine, cobalt blue and prussian blue. The color of the palette should be the same as that of the board you are painting on, so that you can judge how the color will work as you mix it.

Another very useful item for watercolor work is a small piece of natural sponge, which is good for wetting the paper prior to making a wash and also for laying on large washes of color. Other useful things for the art sketching bag are blotting paper, a sharp retractible knife and a water pot. Your sketching set is now fairly comprehensive, but still compact. Having a set like this with you means that you can efficiently achieve a comprehensive and sophisticated result wherever you are.

Oil Paints

Oil painting offers great flexibility, richness and power, and so is a very exciting way to paint the landscape. It is more bulky than watercolor, however, and potentially very messy because it takes a long time to dry, so you have to be fairly well organized.

The first thing you really do need for oil painting is a small sketching easel. Watercolor needs to be painted fairly flat, to avoid drips running down the paper, and so can be done on a small scale on your lap. Oil, however, can be painted in the plane you are looking in, which if you are standing up is vertical. It is therefore more convenient to hold your painting in the same plane, so that you can constantly make comparisons between the painting and the subject. This is what an easel is for and it also has the advantage of leaving both hands free to hold brushes and palette. Avoid using the very brightly colored easels that are available on the market, as these can alter your perception of color in the landscape.

Colors

The colors you choose should give you the broadest range and flexibility, so that you can mix any color you want. Basically if you have the three primary colors, red, yellow and blue, plus white, you will be able to mix all the other colors from them. In practice you need several versions of each color. A practical range would include White, Lemon Yellow, Cadmium Yellow, Cadmium Red, Crimson, Ultramarine Blue, Cobalt Blue and Cerulean Blue; from this selection you will be able to mix most colors. It must be said, however, that this offers a very high key palette. Before about 1800, the only colors normally available were earth colors – brown, earth red, yellow ocher, etc – yet artists achieved bright colorful paintings by relating these lower-key colors brilliantly and getting the maximum contrast between

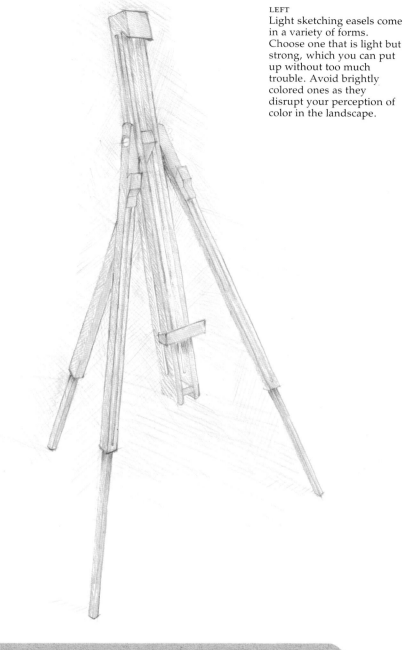

them. It is also possible to achieve more subtle, gentler results with a low key palette of White (Titanium), Lemon Yellow, Yellow Ocher, Venetian Red (Indian Red), Rose Madder, Raw Umber, Burnt Umber, Ultramarine Blue and Cobalt Blue. I generally recommend the higher-key palette because it offers more flexibility and makes the painter think about and work out the color that is actually needed.

Brushes

Brushes used for oil paint should be bristle or hog's hair, especially when you are painting with fairly thick, direct, impressionist brushstrokes, which is generally the most expedient way of painting *'plein air'* (out of doors). This is a stiffer, coarser hair than that used for watercolor and it holds the thicker oil paint more effectively. Applying paint with this type of brush leaves ridge marks, thus increasing the surface area of the dab of paint and making it appear a richer color. You should have a selection of different size brushes for small oil sketching, ranging from 4 to 10 in both round and flat types. Remember also to have several brushes of the same size, so that each can be loaded with a different color and used to produce the same type of mark in the painting without your having to keep cleaning out a favored brush.

Soft brushes are also used for oil paint, especially when painting in glazes. This is where fine translucent layers of oil paint are laid over one another, producing beautiful, subtle and rich effects. This method of oil painting is slower than the direct one, as each layer has to dry. It is not appropriate to *plein air* painting, which is normally done in one sitting, although it is worth having a small selection of soft sable-like brushes in

the paint box for making a greater variety of marks and for delicate brushwork. Oil paint brushes generally have long handles, enabling the painter to work at the easel from a certain distance. An arm's length plus brush length gives you a longer view of both painting and subject, so that you can see how the colors and tones are working together to produce the image. It is interesting to note that Thomas Gainsborough (1727-88), when painting his large studio portrait compositions, used 6-foot long brushes to enable him to stand back far enough to see the image whilst painting.

Palette and Palette Knife

A palette is essential for mixing colors. It should be a flat board with a thumb hole, to allow you to hold it securely in the crook of your arm. For outdoors, rectangular palettes are the most convenient, as they offer the largest surface area that will fit in a rect-

ABOVE AND RIGHT
Kimm Stevens
Flatford Mill after Constable
Oil on canvas, 40 × 50 inches (102.4 × 128 cm)
This series shows the development from an exploratory line drawing, through scaling up and the laying down of a red tonal under-painting, to the full realization of color and detail in a copy of a formidable painting. The tonal monochrome stage is in red-earth (burnt sienna), which complements the cool greens and blues as they are placed upon it. Making such a copy is an extremely revealing and constructive exercise and is probably the best way to gain an insight into the way another artist works.

BELOW
Kimm Stevens
Tree 1
Oil on board, 10 × 14 inches (25.6 × 35.8 cm)

angular paintbox. Palettes do admittedly look a bit ostentatious and beginners can feel a little self-conscious when using one in public, but the design has been perfected over generations of artists and, for sheer convenience and efficiency in mixing colors, is hard to beat. A modern and economical variation on the basic palette is a tear-off greaseproof paper pad, which can be cleaned up by tearing of the soiled top sheet ready for the next session.

Palettes are available in white or a

LEFT
Kimm Stevens
Norfolk Seascape
Oil on board, 10 × 14 inches
(25.6 × 35.8 cm)

LEFT
Kimm Stevens
Norfolk Seascape
Oil on board, 10 × 14 inches
(25.6 × 35.8 cm)

BELOW
Geoff Humphreys
Cotswold Scarp
Oil on board, 15 × 18 inches
(38.4 × 46 cm)

RIGHT
This wonderful device
combines paintbox with
easel, and also provides a
means of carrying wet
pictures, a constant
problem when painting
landscapes. Its main
disadvantage is that it is a
bit heavy and may wobble
if the legs are made too
thin.

BELOW RIGHT
Geoff Humphreys
Morning Landscape
Oil on board, 15 × 18 inches
(38.4 × 46 cm)
This is painted on a red
ground, which sets up a
complementary relationship
with the greens that are
painted over it.

mahogany color; this is not purely an aesthetic choice, but relates to the colored ground (see page 30) on which you paint. Landscape painters often paint on a browny/red board, and a red mahogany palette enables you, as you mix the colors, to see how they will relate to each other in the painting. If you wish to work on a white ground, a white palette is more appropriate.

A palette knife is essential for mixing colors on the palette. These come in a variety of different shapes and sizes; I find that a smallish trowel-shape is very useful for fieldwork. A set of two screw-top dippers that clip to the palette offers a supply of medium (linseed oil) and solvent (turpentine or white/mineral spirit) to enable you to alter the consistency and flow of the paint while mixing. A jar with a tightly fitting screw-top lid, filled with white spirit for cleaning out brushes, and a soft cotton rag completes the basic equipment needed for oil painting.

Paintbox

All this equipment needs some kind of box to carry it in. The classic painting box is a wooden case about 14×18×3 inches, the most luxurious being lined with tin. Although these are a bit heavy, they are very convenient as they hold everything including the palette. Variations on this basic art box include those with devices attached to carry wet paintings, and very complex (and expensive) boxes combined with an easel, which unfolds to become a work surface, easel and paintbox all in one. A simple paintbox can be made cheaply at home with a minimum of carpentry skills.

Acrylic Paints

The other medium which is good for fieldwork is acrylic paint, which in some ways combines the positive, opaque properties of oil paint with the more delicate washes and glazes of watercolor. The basic set of colors needed is the same as for other media. The advantage of acrylic painting, but in some ways also the disadvantage, is that, being water-based, it dries quickly and is then waterproof, so a painting can be built up quickly in layers and changes can be made with ease. Delicate washes can be laid over thick impasto paint in a matter of minutes. Acrylic is particularly compatible with drawing materials and so acts as a robust bridge between the discipline of drawing and painting.

The basic equipment for acrylic painting is the same as for oil painting: you will need an easel and the same set of primary colors (see page 31). Because of acrylic's wide range of properties, brushes can either be bristle or the soft sable type, depending on the final consistency that you wish to achieve. I find a firm, synthetic, chisel-shaped brush is both positive and sensitive to acrylic paints and I would suggest that you include a variety of these in the paint set.

A word of caution about acrylic paint: because it dries so quickly, it is inevitable that the paintbrush gets clogged with dry paint around the ferule (the metal part of the brush in which the hairs are wedged), which tends to splay the hairs and renders the brush useless. This process can be delayed by keeping the brushes wet at all times while painting, and by scrupulously cleaning the brushes in detergent at the end of each session. Damage is inevitable, however, so do not use expensive sable brushes for acrylic painting; stay with the cheaper synthetic type.

The problem of acrylic paint drying so quickly, which is a particular headache on a hot day in the landscape, can be allayed in

two ways. The first is by adding a retardant to the colors as you mix them, which can be purchased in any art shop; the second is by mixing the colors on a special 'Sta Wet' palette, which is a plastic tray with a lid, containing wet blotting paper covered with a

ABOVE
Sally Dray
Dylan's Boathouse
Acrylic, 14 × 24 inches (35.8 × 61.4 cm)

special tissue, on to which you can mix your colors. When the tray is closed, it acts as a micro-climate and keeps the paint wet for several days. In the process of mixing, the paint draws moisture through the liner and stays wet. The specially prepared blotting paper liners and tissues can be obtained at art shops. If you prefer not to accumulate too much special equipment, any shallow suitably sized plastic box with a tight-fitting lid will serve as a substitute for the Sta wet palette.

Survival Equipment

In addition to the set of paints and drawing equipment, which should fit into a small backpack or paintbox, you will need to take into consideration other practicalities when you are out painting the landscape for long periods of time; even on quite warm days you can become cold when you are sitting or standing immobile for long periods of time. Equip yourself with sweaters, a raincoat and fingerless gloves. A hat with a wide brim is useful, both for keeping the rain off, and for shading your eyes from the sun and reducing glare, which can make painting on sultry days very tiring. Do not wear sunglasses, as these reduce the impact of colors and tonal values. A thermos of hot tea or coffee is an essential item as it keeps you both warm and sane when things start to go wrong.

Landscape in the Studio

All the above items of equipment, although pared down to the basic minimum for fieldwork, are adequate for use in the studio (or kitchen table) at home. The beauty of working indoors from sketches made in the field is that you have time to consider what it was that excited you about the particular view, and then have the time and space to experiment with composition, color and media to achieve that idea. The biggest piece of equipment that you need at home is a space where

ABOVE
Sketchbook watercolor

LEFT
Kimm Stevens
Yorkshire Road
Pastel, 22 × 30 inches (56.3 × 76.8 cm)
The watercolor sketch above was done immediately after returning from an evening walk in the Pennines. The hills seemed to merge with the sky, snow and clouds being interchangeable; it was an exciting and powerful image of a hard landscape. The sketch was later developed into the pastel, where the physical gestures possible with charcoal emphasize the energy and the raw power that the landscape had on that cold, late winter's evening.

FAR LEFT
Sally Dray
Cornish Landscape
Acrylic, 16 × 20 inches (41 × 51 cm)
Acrylic paint can be built up in opaque areas, or in very fine washes. In Sally Dray's paintings, both approaches have been used. The surface of the painting is established with fairly firm, decisive passages, which have then been modified with washes and glazes to produce the final subtle effect. Acrylic dries flatter than oil so that the appearance is drier and less luminous, an effect that has value in its own right.

you can set your easel up without being disturbed every five minutes. If you are lucky, that will be a whole room but, even if it is only a tabletop or cupboard, try to allocate it exclusively to painting, so that you can quite easily leave your work out undisturbed, without the great effort of setting up each time. You will find that you will be able to make amazing progress on a painting even in short snatched moments of time, if you can arrange a work space in this way.

Pastels

The other medium that I want to discuss, and which is probably more conveniently used in the studio although it is quite feasible to use it outside, is chalk pastel. Pastels consist of pure pigment bound lightly with gum and rolled into sticks. As a medium, they offer the directness of drawing plus the color of painting. They can be mixed, by blending the colors together on the paper and by layering different colors on to each other, but it is vastly preferable to have as many different colors and tints readily available in the set. This is why pastel sets so quickly become quite large and unwieldy. You should have, as a basic set, warm and

cool versions of red, yellow, blue, green and purple. This gives you ten basic colors. Then you should have at least three to four tints – that is, progressively lighter versions of each color – thus making a set of 30 to 40 colors. Several sticks of white, for adjusting the tones on the paper, complete the set.

This set will give you a very wide range of color and tone, and enable you to make decisions about tones and colors by choosing the most appropriate pastel, rather than by mixing different shades haphazardly on the paper. A stiff bristle brush is used for manipulating the pigment dust around the paper, and fixative spray (aerosol or diffuser) is essential for preserving the drawing, as it is literally made up of particles of unbound pigment and should be given a light coating of fixative when finished. It is unhealthy to breathe in the dust from the pigment in pastels, so it is advisable to wear a lightweight mask, especially if you get a bit physical and excited when drawing.

Another type of pastel is oil pastel, which is pigment bound with an oily wax. The colors are limited and very crude, but beautiful effects and colors can be obtained if they are dissolved on the paper with white/mineral spirit.

ABOVE
Kimm Stevens
Mottistone Down
Pastel, 24 × 36 inches (61.4 × 92.2 cm)
Pastel drawings do not have to be light pale colors; make sure that you have saturated pastels in your set, as well as tints, and you can obtain a very full tonal as well as color range.

RIGHT
Kimm Stevens
Golden Gate
Pastel, 22 × 30 inches (56 × 76.8 cm)
By balancing warm and cool blues and grays of similar tints, you can build up a strong sense of space. Combining this with positive local color and perspective creates a bold drawing which conveys information by means of tone and color.

Grounds

The other crucial area of equipment is the surface on which you paint. This can be paper, board or canvas, depending on the type of work you wish to do.

Papers

Paper is available in a huge variety of textures and weights and it really is up to the individual to experiment and decide which suits their purposes best. In drawing, generally speaking, the smoother papers are good for line drawings, where a rough surface would blur the purity of the line. More textured papers are good for tonal work, especially charcoal and pastel. The textured paper abrades the charcoal or pastel stick, allowing it to transfer the pigment to the paper more efficiently, and a larger quantity of the pigment dust can be held in the ridges of the textured paper, thus producing richer colors and tones.

Pure watercolor requires fairly thick, rough, white paper. The white paper is integral to the painting as it acts as the light in the painting. Tones and colors are achieved

by laying thin glazes over one another which allow the white paper to glow through, thus giving luminosity to the painting. The paper needs to be rough (referred to in art shops as NOT as opposed to HP) so that it holds a satisfactory amount of pigment. The rougher the paper, the richer the colors can become. A fairly heavyweight paper of 140

ABOVE
Barge sketch.

Boards

gsm is convenient for watercolor, as it will not buckle when it gets wet. Lighter papers can be used but they will have to be stretched. This is done by soaking the paper briefly in water, laying it flat on a drawing board and, while it is still wet, sticking it down all around the edges with two-inch brown paper tape, and allowing it to dry flat. The wet, swollen, paper shrinks as it dries out, so it tightens like a drum and becomes a totally flat surface to work on. Stretching is necessary for light watercolor paper and cartridge paper, and offers a good ground for both watercolors and acrylics.

Papers also come in different colors and tones, which are especially useful when using pastel as it allows you to judge the tonal value of the colors as you apply them. Once again be prepared to experiment, but a very effective use of colored grounds is to select the complementary to the prevailing color of the subject; for example, if the landscape is predominantly green, try drawing it on a warm, browny-red paper.

Boards

For oil paint and acrylic you need a more substantial surface, either a board or a stretched canvas. Simple, ready-prepared painting boards can be purchased fairly inexpensively from art shops and are perfectly adequate, though you should select 'canvas boards', which have muslin glued to the surface.

Hardboard is a very stable ground which can be cut to any size, but it must be thoroughly sealed to stop it absorbing the oil out of the paint. A good acrylic primer or dilute PVA glue is perfectly adequate for the job. Use the smooth side of the hardboard for painting on and avoid the machined textured side; being machined, it has an unremittingly mechanical surface which will dominate all the marks you make when painting. If you require a more textural surface, glue muslin on to the smooth side of the board with PVA, allow it to dry, then paint on two coats of white acrylic primer and you will achieve a beautiful working surface.

Larger boards (over 18 inches wide) need to be supported by a frame of 2×1 inch battening attached to the back. The joinery for this is fairly simple; use half lap joints or miters, or even butt joints reinforced by a plate at each corner. The board is then glued

ABOVE
Kimm Stevens
Windy Day
Oil on board, 10 × 14 inches (25.6 × 35.8 cm)
This was painted in a short time, the main aim being to capture the freshness of color and light. You can achieve a freshness of paint surface by painting so quickly, but you must concentrate hard in order to keep to the point and know to stop when you have shown what you intended.

RIGHT
Geoff Humphries
The Apple Tree
Oil on board, 18 × 24 inches (46 × 61.4 cm)

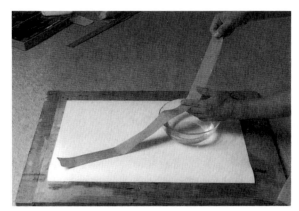

The process of stretching paper.

FAR LEFT
Prepare a clean drawing board, a sheet of watercolor paper, four pieces of two-inch gumstrip paper cut slightly longer than the paper edges, a bowl of water and a sponge.

LEFT
Wet the back of the paper evenly, using the sponge, and lay it face up on the board; the paper should bubble up slightly.

FAR LEFT
Damp the gumstrip by running it through the water or wiping it with the wet sponge.

LEFT
Tape all the edges of the dampened paper to the board and allow it to dry flat. The paper will stretch as it dries because it is anchored by the gumstrip. Leave it attached to the board as you paint and you will have a fine and stable surface on which to paint watercolors.

and nailed to the battens with hardboard nails, the nailheads being pushed below the surface and the holes filled, before you prime it with two to three coats of acrylic primer.

Canvas

The traditional ground for oil painting and still the most convenient, especially for large paintings, is canvas. Canvas was favored as a ground historically because it is relatively light and can be sewn together, so huge paintings are feasible. It can also be rolled, so transportation of huge paintings is easy. Canvas has a delightful texture to paint on and there are many different types and prices; once again you should experiment and choose the type that suits you best. Canvas is a fairly unstable surface to work on, however; being a woven material, it swells and shrinks due to humidity and weather. It dents, it rots and it is highly absorbent.

Canvas also needs careful preparation. Ideally it should be mounted on special inter-locking stretchers. A stretcher is a frame with specially-cut corner joints which can be opened by hammering wedges into the corners; this stretches the canvas and keeps it flat and taut. Ready-prepared, primed and stretched canvas can be purchased from art shops and this is obviously the most convenient, though most expensive, way to start. Canvas also needs to be carefully sealed and primed, to ensure that the oil paint cannot penetrate and rot the material. Two or three coats of proprietary acrylic primer does this job perfectly well.

The traditional method of preparing a canvas for oil painting involves, first, attaching the canvas to the stretcher, nailing down the center of one side, then the center of the opposite side, followed by the centers of the other two sides, while keeping the canvas under tension at all times. Work along each side toward the corners, maintaining an even strain across the stretcher. At the corners, make a folded tuck to ensure that there are no creases as the canvas turns, and make sure that the interlocking miter joint is not nailed together. Once the canvas is stretched, you should paint hot rabbit-skin glue size on both sides and allow it to dry, applying two further coats to the front of the canvas. The purpose of the rabbit-skin glue is to seal the canvas from any paint. Once this is dry, two coats of good-quality oil-based undercoat should be applied, to build up the surface and provide a sound base for painting. This is quite an arduous process,

but it is very satisfying to do and gives the best ground for an oil painting.

Camera

The final piece of equipment that is extremely useful for collecting information in the field is a camera. If the camera is used in conjunction with drawings and paintings, it becomes a valuable aid for gathering detailed material and provides a reference and reminder when working in the studio. I am not recommending that you use it as the main reference, for if you copy a photograph of a landscape, you will simply paint a picture of a photograph. Your drawings and paintings are the true key to your ideas and experiences and, ultimately, to your own originality, which should be more interesting than any photograph. The camera's value lies in providing a wealth of detail for reference, and it can freeze movement, which is extremely useful if you are drawing animals, or people on the move. Any camera will do, but the most universal is an SLR camera, preferably with a zoom lens, giving you greater flexibility in framing the picture that you want. Polaroid cameras are especially useful if you need to refer instantly to a photograph while drawing, to help you capture a fleeting moment or movement.

LEFT
Three simple joints for preparing corners when battening a hardboard panel.
(i) A simple butt joint, which is glued and strengthened by nailing a plate or triangle of hardboard across the back.
(ii) A miter, which is neater and can be nailed diagonally through the miter to prevent the joint opening up should it be twisted.
(iii) A half lap joint, which takes a little more time and measuring, but provides much more strength and rigidity to the panel, and is neater as it needs no reinforcement.
Once the frame is made, the hardboard is glued and nailed on to it, which makes the whole panel very rigid. The nails should be punched below the surface of the board and the holes filled. The edges should be sanded or planed so they are flush with the battening and then the whole board should be lightly sanded, ready for priming.

ABOVE RIGHT
Kimm Stevens
Standing Stone
Charcoal, 22 × 30 inches (56.3 × 76.8 cm)
When making an ambitious drawing on site, you have all the information in front of you to select from and can distill the experience of the place while you are there.

RIGHT
Jim Lee
Landscape with Greenhouse
Oil on board, 24 × 36 inches (61.4 × 92.1 cm)
Built on a strong diagonal, this picture carries the eye up and across the canvas, to be stopped by the end of the field, which forces the eye down the tree to the left and back up the diagonal thrust of the greenhouse.

3. Drawing

Drawing is the action of making a mark on paper; various marks create a pattern, which can be harmonious or discordant. The totally magical thing about drawing is that the marks which combine to make pattern and rhythm can be organized so as to fool the brain into thinking that it is looking at something that is not there. It can create an illusion of reality. Show any person a picture of a vase of flowers and they will say 'It's a vase of flowers'; but it isn't, it's a load of paint smeared very cleverly on a piece of canvas.

This trick, this illusion, has been developed, discussed, changed, formalized over the entire history of civilization, with different cultures developing different methods and systems. The artist can absorb these systems and can use them as the basic mechanics of creating illusion in drawing. In the twentieth century, painters have looked to many cultures and developed new drawing systems, but the most fundamental and powerful system of creating an illusion of reality, and the most common in Western civilization, is perspective drawing.

Perspective

Perspective is a geometric system which takes account of the fact that objects appear to diminish in size as they get further away,

and that the eye level of the viewer coincides with the point at which the objects recede to nothing. In its simplest form, the sides of the top of a cube, seen head on, will recede to a point that coincides with the viewer's eye level. You can demonstrate this to yourself by performing a simple exercise. Sit directly in front of a rectangular object, say a table,

look straight ahead through one eye and locate a point on the wall opposite which is in direct horizontal alignment with your eye. Do this by placing a sharp pencil very close to your eyeball so that you can see the point as you look ahead. Make a mark on the wall where that point comes; this point is the center of your vision. It should be exactly the same height from the ground as your eye is if you are sitting up straight. Now take two long pencils and with one in each hand hold them vertical and very close to your face, keeping one eye shut, adjust the pencils, keeping them vertical, so that they run up the sides of the table. The pencils should form two sides of a triangle whose apex coincides with the mark you made on the wall. Any other line in the room that is parallel to the sides of the table, say a skirting board or the corner of the ceiling, will also extend up or down to this point. Try it and see! If you stand up and perform the same exercise, the lines will recede to a new higher horizon that again coincides with the height your eye is from the ground. This demonstrates basic single-point perspective and the critical relationship between horizon and eye level.

Obviously we do not see the world conveniently from a head-on view, so a more useful development from the basic single-viewpoint perspective is two-point perspective, allowing an object to be presented at an angle to the viewer. The basic criteria still apply; each side of the object recedes in different directions, and lines that are parallel to each other in real life recede to the vanishing point. All lines recede to the same level, the horizon. Again, if the eye level changes, so do the angles of recession. This has huge implications in landscape painting because it enables you to establish different senses of

space, be it a crowded urban scene or a great open vista seen from a mountain top.

There is a third element of perspective which occurs in very large objects, such as buildings, which is that they recede both

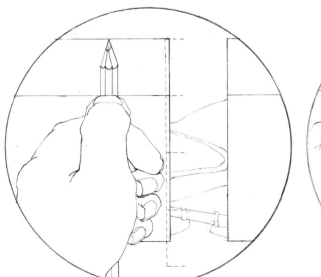

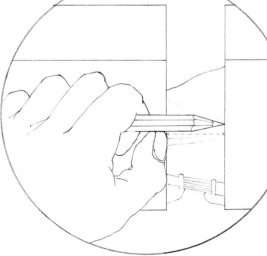

ABOVE
Kimm Stevens
Backyard 1
Charcoal, 30 × 22 inches
(76.8 × 56.5 cm)

LEFT
Holding the pencil at arm's length, measure off a chosen dimension, using the point of the pencil and the thumb, and see how many times that distance goes into another dimension in the view; in this case, the gap between the two buildings is compared with the height of the building on the left.

FAR LEFT
Ginny Chalcraft
Cumbrian Stream
Conté and pastel, 11½ × 32¼ inches (29.4 × 82.5 cm)
This drawing uses line to build up textures and tones simultaneously into a delightful study of trees and water.

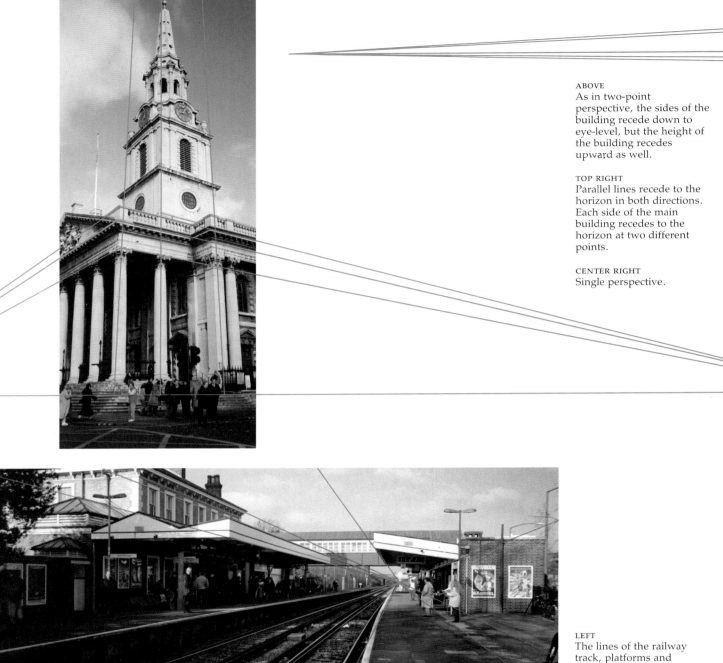

ABOVE
As in two-point perspective, the sides of the building recede down to eye-level, but the height of the building recedes upward as well.

TOP RIGHT
Parallel lines recede to the horizon in both directions. Each side of the main building recedes to the horizon at two different points.

CENTER RIGHT
Single perspective.

LEFT
The lines of the railway track, platforms and buildings, are all parallel to each other and all recede to one central vanishing point, on the horizon or at eye-level.

from side to side and upward or downward. This is known as three-point perspective and reflects the fact that the viewer is looking up at an angle rather than dead ahead, where all the vertical lines are parallel.

A grasp of these basic elements of perspective will enable you to understand and anticipate how certain lines help to create a feeling of space and volume. The angles of lines in the landscape become crucial and often relate to the horizon and the viewer's eye level. Direct observation is the critical element of landscape painting; to gain a sense of space you need to develop ways of making sure that you are drawing what you

see rather than what you think you see. This objective approach gives you control, greater understanding of what you are looking at and, ultimately, greater freedom to express your ideas with originality, because you have collected the information first-hand from nature itself.

Scale and Space

One of the most surprising things in the landscape is how dramatically scale changes as the distance increases and how often we alter that scale, depending on what importance we place on particular features. If you

RIGHT
Ginny Chalcraft
View of the Town Square and South Gateway
Conté, wash and line, 14 × 21 inches (36 × 54 cm)
Perspective distance is enhanced by the dark framework of the arch, which provides the eye with an intriguing entry into the picture. Tone is provided by the application of washes of watercolor, which are then reinforced with pen and ink. Though pastel, the picture is predominantly monotone, relying on tone rather than color to build the form.

Town Square

On entering Town Square, one finds a tranquil, dignified place, surrounded by tall mellow brick and stucco buildings in the Georgian style. The grey pitched roofs abound with squat dormer windows, like little sentry boxes. At each corner, the roofs boast an ornamental cupola. Bossy towers with golden balls, weather vanes and spires. But not only are they diverse and beautiful, they are extremely functional as they provide housing units for the air-conditioning plant.

The curved arch of the South Gateway framing the view of the river beyond.

Try looking at the
landscape, not as separate
trees and buildings, but as
the shapes that those
objects make between each
other. If the photograph
represents the basic
landscape, the outline of
the shapes between the
trees emphasizes the
particular relationships
between them and creates a
drawing that is both
confident and original.

are impressed by a certain building or
natural feature, it is very easy to emphasize
its importance by making it too big in the picture. While there is nothing intrinsically
wrong in doing this – indeed many cultures
use scale to emphasize importance – the
effect of it is to destroy the sense of space
within the picture, which may foil your
original intentions. A sense of scale can be
maintained by constantly measuring and
comparing the dimensions of different
features and shapes within the landscape
itself.

The very simplest and most direct way of
seeing and drawing the actual scale of the
subject is to trace a view on to a piece of
glass. Take a felt-tip pen and stand at a window looking out. Close one eye and, keeping your head very still, trace on the glass all
the lines and shapes that you can see. Do not
worry what each line is, just trace them all.
You should, in a very short time, have made
a drawing that has a very strong sense of
space and scale. When doing this, see how
small, near objects, say a leaf on a nearby
plant, compare in scale to distant, large
objects, like buildings or cars. Often what

we perceive as small turns out to be com-
paratively much bigger than what logic tells
us we should accept as large. Not only does
this exercise demonstrate the radical
changes of scale that exist between objects
over different distances, but it also forces
you to translate the three-dimensional space
of reality into a two-dimensional illusion on
a pane of glass, by drawing space and
objects as a series of flat shapes that fit together like a jigsaw puzzle.

Once this idea has been grasped, it is a
small step to making a drawing. Seeing
objects as shapes enables you to depict them
as they actually are and not as you think they
are. Seeing shapes also enables you to
appreciate the relationships and spaces between objects, so that you are no longer
looking at objects which float around in a
void, but are looking at the relationships between the objects and the space that they
occupy. The drawing rebuilds the specific
momentary reality that presents itself, and
you have a wonderful opportunity to capture and fix the harmony and beauty of
those relationships, which are unique and
totally original.

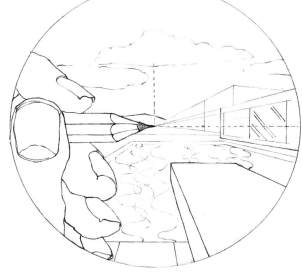

On the bridge is the
riverside frontage of neo-classical buildings
like the elegant facade with its mixture
Finely conserved historical townscape. But of course

Measuring

There are several methods and devices to help you see the shapes you are observing as they actually are, and drawing on glass is an extremely good demonstration. Accurate measuring also helps you to check your decisions and is a very simple procedure. I suggest that you draw first, then check your initial, instinctive response, rather than measuring it all up first, which can make the drawing rather mechanical. To measure, take a pencil and hold it out at arm's length vertically, parallel to the plane of your face. Select a shape from the view that you wish to investigate, say the proportion of the gap between two buildings. Now, taking the pencil

ABOVE
Ginny Chalcraft
The Riverside
Pen and wash with gouache, 14 × 21 inches (36 × 54 cm)
Strong linear perspective and dramatic contrasts of scale create a powerful statement about the neo-classical architecture of Richmond, Surrey.

LEFT
Hold the point of the pencil close to one eye, with the other eye closed, so that it appears in the center of your vision. The point will coincide with the horizon and your eye-level, and marks the level to which all parallel lines will recede.

LEFT
Ginny Chalcraft
*Steps by Tower House,
Richmond*
Pastel, 14 × 21 inches (36 ×
54 cm)

RIGHT
Holding pencils parallel to
your face, and using only
one eye, line the pencils up
along each side of a
rectangular object going
away from you. Where the
pencils cross will coincide
with your eye-level and the
horizon, and establish the
vanishing point of that
rectangle.

and holding it, once again, at arm's length, keeping it parallel to your face and horizontal, line up the tip of the pencil with the side of one building. Slide your finger along the pencil until it coincides with the side of the other building, and you now have a measurement of the width of the shape. Keeping your finger firmly on the measured position on the pencil, turn the pencil vertical, line up with the bottom of the shape and see how many times your width measurement goes into the height. This rather fiddly process helps you to see and compare pro-

portion and scale. It is useful to take the initial measurement and compare it with other shapes and lines throughout the drawing, so as to maintain a constant check.

The other area to keep a constant check upon is the angles of lines and their relationship to each other. A line will only appear to be at an angle if it is relating to another line, be that the side of the drawing or a line within the drawing. Furthermore, if all the angles in a drawing are correct, the drawing will automatically be in proportion, so devising a way to check angles is very useful. A

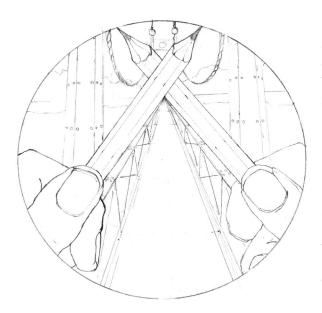

spatial way. While measuring systems are very useful to get a result, and help us see what we are looking at, they alone will not be able to generate the energy and excitement that you will engender when you embrace the full possibilities and problems of objective drawing.

Tone

Seeing the world in terms of shapes relating to each other, and gaining skills in drawing those shapes with line, gives a very strong basis for all drawing, painting and composition. Once you have observed the shapes, you can observe the effect of light on them, and develop the idea of form and space not just with line, but with light and dark, or tone. Tonal drawing relates much more directly to the way we see than does line. A line is a fairly abstract way of depicting the world; lines simply mark the boundaries of change where one area changes to another. Tone is what happens in these areas, so tone changes where lines in a drawing occur. Our eyes have evolved to respond to light and dark, and we perceive and understand our surroundings by decoding the information

simple plumbline made from a piece of string, with a weight tied to the end, suspended from the side of the easel in such a way that it cuts through your view, will establish an absolute vertical with which you can compare other angles in the subject.

A less cumbersome, though less accurate, way to help you see angles, which I use, is simply to hold your pencil up and close to your face, in front of your eye, and align it along the line that you are investigating. The pencil becomes a huge line traveling at the given angle and emphasizes the angle, forcing you to see it (see illustration, page 51). If you are working at an easel, you can gently swing your body around to your drawing, while holding the pencil at the observed angle, and compare the measured angle with the corresponding line in the drawing, in order to make a rough check. It is surprising how easy it is to get the angles of lines going completely the wrong way, so a check is very useful.

All these measuring systems require you to look through one eye. This is because looking through one eye simplifies the information going to the brain, and having only one viewpoint tends to flatten the space. Looking through both eyes, we constantly compute the information from two sources so that our spatial sense is really very sophisticated. It is interesting that animals which have a crucial need to judge distance to survive, whether to leap from branch to branch or pounce on some unsuspecting prey, all have this binocular vision. When drawing, binocular vision tends to add confusion to the need to flatten real space into two dimensions, but the fact remains that we do have binocular vision and see the world in a more dynamic and

BELOW
Kimm Stevens
Sketchbook
Pencil, 6 × 8 inches (15 × 20 cm)
This careful line drawing, done on a rainy day, explores the selective scale of objects over a distance. The stones on the wall are a comparable size to the more distant tower.

contained in the light and dark around us. We need both light and dark to do this. If we only have dark we see nothing (it's dark)! Conversely if everything is flooded with light from all directions, we again find it difficult to orientate ourselves. Ideally, we should have one really powerful light source, which casts light from one direction, thus illuminating one side of the form and casting a shadow on the other side. Fortunately, the landscape has one such light source: the sun.

Sunlight provides infinite variations of light, depending on the atmosphere and time of day and season. In the morning and evening, the sun is low in the sky and casts long, dramatic shadows; at noon, it is high in the sky and illuminates all round the form, casting less shadow and tending visually to flatten everything. If there is a lot of moisture in the air, the sunlight is diffused and loses its strong directional dynamic, softening all the tones. An extreme of this is fog, where the light is so diffused by water droplets that no tone reflected from any object can get through

directly to your eye and you see very little. The time of year also changes the quality of sunlight. In winter in the northern hemisphere, the sun is low in the sky and weaker and therefore casts longer shadows; colors are subdued. In summer, the sun is high and strong and we get bright colors and stronger shadows.

The height of the sun in the sky relates directly to the shadows cast. In the morning and evening, the sun casts long shadows which help to show form more directly and dramatically. The length of the shadow can be determined geometrically by projecting the angle of the sun to the horizon, through the object on to the ground beyond.

Sunlight not only casts shadows but illuminates the whole landscape, because it is diffused by the molecules in the atmosphere. On a bright day we are aware of a strong directional light, but less aware that most of the light has been diffused into a blanket of light that illuminates things more easily (on the moon, where there is no atmosphere, the sky is perpetually black and daylight only illuminates the rocks that it

FAR RIGHT
Kimm Stevens
Backyard II
Charcoal, 30 × 22 inches (77 × 56 cm)
This drawing exploits the contrast of black and white across the picture plane, sometimes referring to the light source, sometimes emphasizing the local color of the object. The result is an immediate, strong visual impact.

BELOW
Kimm Stevens
Barge
Charcoal, 22 × 30 inches (56 × 72 cm)
Taking a low eyelevel and drawing against the light emphasizes the scale and drama of the subject. Uncompromising use of black and white allows the medium its full range in order to achieve the luminosity required when drawing the direct light source.

falls upon). This even blanket of light sets up another basic tonal relationship within the landscape. The sun, generally being above the landscape, casts more light on horizontal surfaces and less on vertical surfaces, so fields and roads and the land will often be lighter than the trees, hedges and buildings that stand upon it, regardless of their color. However, tops of trees and buildings will receive a similar level of light and will relate more to the horizontal land.

Just as in a line drawing, where space is shown by relating one shape to another, so a tonal drawing can only work if one area of tone relates to others right across the drawing. The lightest light that you have in drawing is the white paper, the darkest tone you can get is black, so you have to use these two extremes to create the relationships that exist between sunlight and landscape. You can only make an area bright and light by exploiting the darker ones which surround it. To help you see tonal differences, it is helpful to view the scene through half-closed eyes; this reduces the color and halftones and emphasizes the lightest and darkest areas.

In this chapter I have attempted to show various approaches to drawing, and how to use drawing as a means to greater understanding of the landscape. A systematic and measured approach to drawing enables you to understand and control the very complex problem of translating real space on to a two-dimensional plane. Understanding perspective, light and tone will allow you to anticipate certain natural events and phenomena as they occur. Drawing, however, is more than this. Once the basic elements and principles of the language have been absorbed – and I personally believe that this is essential if you want other people to understand what you say – they provide a route for a rich exploration of media, composition and rhythm, which can provide the individual with a powerful means of expression. Drawing is an invaluable tool as well as a skill in its own right.

BELOW
Ginny Chalcraft
Topiary
Conté crayon, 11½ × 32½ inches (29 × 83 cm)
Here the light and dark relationships between trees and lawns create space and form.

4. Color

We now come to the most immediate and important element in landscape painting, color. Light plays an essential role in the way we see the world; in fact our eyes do not respond to objects, but to the light reflected off them. We do not see trees, grass, etc., but light that has bounced off these things and traveled into our eye. Sky is inevitably brighter than land, because the light has only been diffused by the air and is fairly complete. When the light hits a tree, a lot more of it is dispersed and absorbed by the tree, so that less bounces back and the tree appears darker. The passage of the light is broken and disturbed in many different ways, by being dispersed, reflected, absorbed, refracted and blocked, and this leads to the infinity of different conditions and effects that nature offers.

The Effect of Light on Objects

Newton demonstrated that light from the sun is made up of the colors of the rainbow, by splitting the white sunlight through a prism, slowing the rays at different rates through the different thicknesses of the glass, and then reassembling them to white light by passing them through another prism.

Different surfaces and textures reflect and respond to light in different ways. A mirror, for instance, reflects the rays of light so faithfully that we can see a complete image of where the light has come from, be it the light source, or other surfaces from which the light has reflected. A white surface is less reflective than a mirror and does not reflect individual images, but it does reflect a lot of light, most of it in fact, and white appears to be light. If you paint a room all white, especially if you include the floor, the room appears to be incredibly light. A piece of black velvet, however, appears to be very dark. A black surface, especially if its texture is not smooth, absorbs light, so appearing dark or black. If, on a sunny day, you feel the bodywork of a white car and a black car, you will find that the white car is cooler because the lighter color has reflected the light energy, whereas the black car has absorbed the light energy, which causes the surface to heat up.

The fact that different surfaces reflect or absorb light in different ways is crucial to gaining a full appreciation of the nature of color. A surface that appears to us as a parti-

BELOW
Clova Stuart-Hamilton
Dordogne Bathers
Watercolor, 12 × 16 inches (31 × 41 cm)
Figures emerge from the brushwork through the complementary warms of the skin tone reacting with the cool blues and greens of the surrounding landscape.

RIGHT
Kimm Stevens
Esher Common
Pastel, 21 × 30 inches (54 × 72 cm)
In this drawing the green-blue is exaggerated, to accommodate the intense red of the autumnal trees and to establish a certain distance by means of aerial perspective. The tree trunks form a grid in front of the color and establish a distance between the foreground and the powerfully red trees.

cular color does so by virtue of the fact that it reflects that color within the light spectrum and absorbs all the other colors. For instance, a red letterbox will reflect the reds in the spectrum that make up white light and absorb the blues, yellows and greens of the spectrum. A blue object will likewise reflect the blues and absorb the yellows, reds and oranges.

A close relationship develops between the light reflected by a colored surface and the light absorbed by that colored surface. In the case of the letterbox, red is reflected, and the mixture of blues, yellows and greens that are absorbed combine to give a green. There is thus a strong relationship of opposites between red and green, which are therefore said to be complementary to each other. If we look at the letterbox in a green light or through a green filter, there is no red in the spectrum of light that we are looking in, so none can be reflected back, but the red surface of the object still absorbs the green of the spectrum, and the object therefore appears to be black, as it absorbs all the available light.

Color and the Eye

Objects have a constant and close relationship with light, and their colors can change depending on the quality and quantity of light available. Our eyes also respond to light and color, and they are the other important factor in the way we perceive color. Just as objects reflect and absorb light, so the retina in the eye responds, compensates for and balances the levels of color and light that fall upon it. Generally, we see colors as they are; in normal conditions they are balanced and we accept the information conveyed by our eyes. If, however, we overstimulate the retina, strange things start to happen. Stare at a red spot for two to three minutes; in doing this you are overstimulating the red response in the retina. Now look away to a blank surface, or simply close your eyes, and you will 'see' a corresponding dot of a beautiful, luminous, greeny-blue, the perfect complementary of the red, because your eyes have been desensitized to red.

This same phenomenon often occurs when a strong color is close to a more neutral

BELOW
Look at the red spot for a few minutes, allowing your eyes to glaze over; the red spot will fluoresce and a halo will appear around it. Once this happens, look away to a neutral blank area, or simply close your eyes, and you will 'see' the complementary color, green.

or less reflective one. Take a bright green square and place in it a neutral gray square of a similar tone. After a short period of looking, the gray square will appear to be a plummy red. Using the same gray square, but with a blue border, the gray will appear to be slightly orange. Our eyes overcompensate in the more neutral areas and 'see' the complementary of the more dominant color, which is desensitizing the retina.

The Effects of Light on the Landscape

Light affects the way you see the landscape all the time, and once you are aware of this it opens up vast possibilities for painting. On a bright, hot, sunny day, the light is warm yellow and orange; it bounces off objects and sends back strong, hot colors to the eye. Where the light does not fall, the eye, overstimulated by the hot colors, starts to see complementary cool colors in the more neutral, less luminous areas; the shadows appear to be blue and violet, the complementary of the warm yellow-orange light source. Obviously these colors are complicated by the local color of the object: a blue shadow cast on grass will become greeny blue as it mixes with the green of the grass. It

is very important to grasp the fact that a strong light sets up colors complementary to itself in the shadows, and it is well worth taking some time to observe and understand

ABOVE
The two grays in the squares on the left are the same as the grays in the squares on the right; they appear to be different because of the influence of the dominant color surrounding them. The eye sees the complementary in the more neutral color. Note that the color and the gray are a similar tone, reducing the light-to-dark contrast, which would diminish the effect of the warm/cool complementary color relationship. This same phenomenon occurs in landscape, when shadows (neutral unlit areas) take on the complementary of the light source, usually warm yellow/orange; thus shadows on a bright day will appear to be bluish purple.

LEFT
Geoff Humphreys
Hay Fields
Oil on board, 14 × 18 inches
(36 × 46 cm)
Note the use of complementary colors in the shadows, especially the use of violet in the hay field.

the depth that this new dimension of color offers.

The less intense the sunlight is, the more the actual (or local) color of the objects – say trees – dominates; in a gray English landscape, there will be more reds (the complementary of green) in the shadows. It is interesting to note that in Constable's sketches, he paints on an earth-red ground, which serves immediately as shadows when strokes of green are placed on it to represent the lit areas of trees.

ABOVE
This diagram emphasizes the relationship between objects, the light source and the eye. It is always useful while painting to think that it is not objects that you are seeing, but light bouncing off the different surfaces, and that you are not painting the objects, but the light. The light from the sun is reflected by objects into the eye; the color of the object is perceived because some of the spectrum is being absorbed by the surface of the object and the residue is reflected.

Aerial Perspective

The other element of landscape which plays an important part in our perception of color is the atmosphere, which represents the vast bulk of any landscape. We usually relate to the terrain and any features which appear upon it, but these are mainly flat or undulating; the really big thing is the huge block of space that exists above the land. We usually refer to this as the 'sky', but this encourages a preconception of a blue plane with clouds dotted about. Try to see it rather as a volume, an entity in itself, albeit a gas rather than rock, which reacts with light in a different way to the more solid, tangible forms that it envelops. The solid forms reflect light; the atmosphere diffuses light, that is, light passes through it but gets redirected as it hits particles of moisture or pollution, which alters its quality and color. An extreme case of this is fog, where the light is so much dispersed by the particles of moisture that any light reflected off an object has been redirected many times, and we see very little of specific objects but rather a haze of white light. The same thing happens when looking over long distances; the further you look the more air and particles of moisture you look through, so the light is more diffused. The warmer slower-wavelength colors, reds and yellows, are dis-

ABOVE
Clova Stuart-Hamilton
*Valley of the Feugh,
Kincardineshire*
Oil on canvas, 13 × 11
inches (33 × 28 cm)

LEFT
The actual color of the
foliage and grass is the
same in the immediate
foreground and on the
distant hills, but the effect
of the atmosphere is to cool
the almost yellow-green of
the foreground down to
blue and violet in the hills.

ABOVE RIGHT
Geoff Humphreys
From the Wolds
Oil on board, 16 × 18 inches
(41 × 46 cm)
The distance in this
painting is established,
almost entirely, by the use
of aerial perspective.

RIGHT
The sun is low in the sky
and the light travels
through a greater thickness
of air to reach the eye, so
that the lower frequencies,
reds and oranges,
dominate.

persed and it is only the higher-frequency colors, blues and violets, that get through, so distant hills appear to be violet and blue in contrast to the warmer colors in the foreground. This is known as aerial or atmospheric perspective and is why cool colors appear to recede and warm colors to advance.

When the sun goes down in the evening, the light has to travel through a greater distance of atmosphere and is slowed down. As a result the slower-frequency colors often dominate and in the evening the sky turns red and yellow. On damp autumnal evenings the effect is magnified by the moisture-laden atmosphere, which acts as a lens and makes the sun appear huge on the horizon.

Light and atmosphere play a huge part in the way we see the landscape. In terms of painting, it is the effect they have on color that is the key. Since shape and color are all that we have in painting, it is to color in painting that we now turn to link nature with landscape.

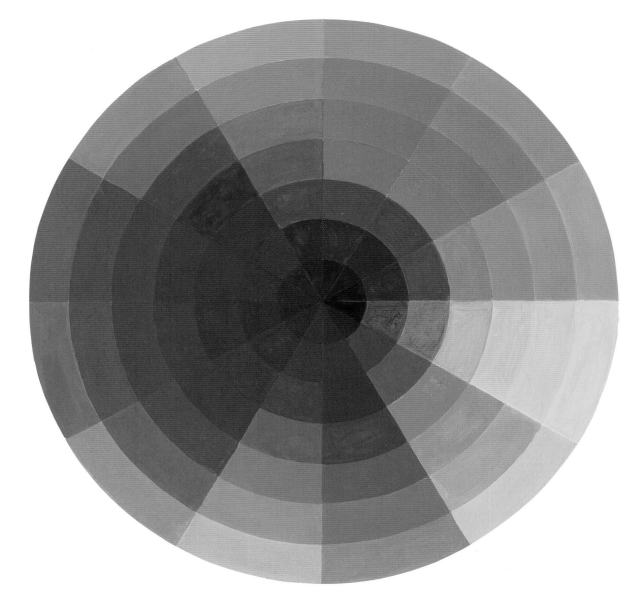

LEFT
It is very useful exercise actually to make this color wheel, as it forces you to mix colors carefully, using only a warm and cool version of the primaries red, yellow and blue. Construct a circle with a radius of 7 inches (18 cm) on a piece of card. Draw six concentric circles at 1 inch (3 cm) intervals toward the center, and then draw radii at 30 degrees to each other from the center, thus producing the twelve segments. The mid-ring is pure saturated color, the outer rings are progressively lighter tints, and the inner rings are the darker tones, which are best achieved by adding carefully judged complementary color in order to absorb the light down to black (NB no actual black was used on this color wheel). The wheel demonstrates the relationships between the complementaries, the cool blue, green, purple opposing the warm orange, red and yellow, and the different tones and tonal ranges of the colors, e.g. yellow is light, blue is dark. Note also how much of the color wheel is green, from the yellow segment right round to the blue segment, a good third of the whole wheel, hence the subtlety of that color.

RIGHT ABOVE
Geoff Humphreys
Green Fields
Oil on board, 14 × 18 inches (36 × 46 cm)

RIGHT BELOW
This diagram demonstrates the varying tonal ranges of four basic colors. The green and blue operate as color from white right through to black, whereas yellow can only be described as yellow from white down to mid-tone yellow; as soon as any dark is added, it becomes brown, and yellow therefore has a limited tonal range. Red is even more restricted tonally, only operating as red in the mid-tone range. If you paint in the tone band that accommodates all the colors, the red will be less likely to 'jump'. To achieve a light red, the colors around it are adjusted to a darker tone.

Color Wheel

Just as colors affect each other in nature, so they do in painting. Once again it is all to do with relationships. A red shape painted on a white ground appears to be dark, while the same red shape on a black ground will appear to be light. It is the relationship of one color to those surrounding it that conveys the idea and intention of the painting. The difference between color in nature and color in painting is that, in nature, when the colors in light identified by Newton are mixed they become white light, but when pigments are all mixed together, as you will soon discover, they become a sludgy, browny-black, because the pigments absorb light. Adding white lightens color, but reduces its intensity. Thus working with pigment has its limitations, which need to be understood in order for color to be used to its maximum effect.

When you are painting there are two color dynamics to work with, light and dark colors, and warm and cool colors. It is very useful at this point to construct a color wheel, where the relationships between colors and their complementaries can be observed. In the color wheel illustrated here, the tonal dynamic, white to black, is integrated with the saturated color dynamic of complementaries and warm and cool. It is important to note that the black center in the darker versions of the colors is achieved by adding carefully judged complementary 'absorbing' colors. These cancel out the reflective color and produce darker versions of the color, until a point of no reflection, or black, is reached in the center. White is added in stages to the original saturated color to produce the lighter tones or tints.

In making the color wheel, you will be able to observe, first, that different saturated colors are of different tones (pure yellow, for instance, is lighter than pure blue); and, second, that colors respond tonally in different ways. Blue still remains blue even when it is very light and when it is very dark;

it remains the same color throughout the tonal range. Red, however, behaves differently; when it gets dark it becomes brown, and when white is added, it becomes pink. Pure red has a very limited mid-tone range. Likewise, yellow operates as yellow when it is mixed with white, but in the darker sections it goes brown and loses its hue, or pure color. Yellow also has a limited tonal range. This limitation on the warm colors, red, orange and yellow, means that they have to be used with some care to balance their tones with the surrounding colors.

If you are painting a red object in the landscape, the surrounding colors have to be adjusted to the required tonal level of the local red color. Otherwise the tonal structure of the painting will be disrupted and the illusion of space destroyed, with the red object appearing to jump out of the picture because the contrast is so great. This is, of course, why the color red stands out in real life; it has such contrast. A true red has a mid to dark tone, which stands out against the generally lighter tones of the landscape. Combined with the fact that the color of the landscape is often green, the complementary of red, this doubles the potential impact and problem of red.

Orange and yellow have similar properties, but because they have a broader tonal range, up to white, they are slightly more flexible and can be balanced more easily. This is one of the main reasons why paintings with flowers in bloom often go very flat; the artist has not recognized and maintained the tonal balance between the hot colored flowers and the green shadowy leaves, and the flowers jump forward, destroying the illusion of space. Of course in nature that is just what the flowers are meant to do, standing out from the foliage in order to attract bees and other insects. It is thus very difficult to maintain the illusion of space, by balancing the tones of the picture according to the light source and then allowing enough color contrast, in order to show the brightness and beauty of the flowers, while still holding them in their place within the illusion of the picture.

The other major problem that landscape painting poses is the use of the color green. If you have any sense at all, you will at this point close the book and take up embroidery, but if not, take your color wheel and observe the fact that the area covered by green extends from the yellow segment through green right round to blue and

ABOVE
Peter Lloyd-Jones
Fordson Major
Oil on canvas, 36 × 40
inches (92 × 102 cm)
A good example of holding
red in place by exploiting
the complementary blue-
green in the bodywork of
the tractor and the
surrounding landscape.

through all the concentric segments from white to black. There are yellow greens, olive greens, bluey greens, and many, many more. In fact, both a cool yellow and a cool blue will appear to be green when placed next to a warmer color. Green has a huge color and tonal range, which must be encompassed in order to grasp the full potential of the color. Look at the landscape not as being green, but as having different levels of yellowness or blueness. Take a small piece of card, about 2″×3″ and punch a small hole in the center, about ¼″ diameter, then select a tree in the middle distance and observe its color through the hole; you have isolated that color. Bring the hole down to a green in the immediate foreground, say the grass at your feet, and observe the difference between the greens; the tree is probably a lot more blue than the grass. These differences can then be exploited in the painting. Even if they are exaggerated, tree shown as blue and grass yellow, the relationship will still work and the illusion of space will exist.

Color Mixing

We turn to the color wheel once again when mixing colors on the palette. Red, yellow and blue are the primary colors, essential for

ABOVE
Clova Stuart-Hamilton
Houses at Born
Watercolor, 13 × 16 inches
(33 × 41 cm)

LEFT
Kimm Stevens
Tree
Oil on board, 9 × 12 inches
(23 × 30 cm)

mixing all the other colors. Mixing any two primaries produces the secondary colors:

    Orange – Red plus Yellow
    Green – Yellow plus Blue
    Purple – Blue plus Red.

If the third primary is added (which is the complementary of the secondary color), it will absorb the initial color and tend to make it darker and less saturated. If blue is added to its complementary, orange, it will produce dull, darker orange or brown. Add more blue, and it will become cooler and grayer. Add white to the mixture, and a full tonal range of grays, beiges and browns becomes possible.

Once you have absorbed the initial idea that any color can be mixed by balancing the three primaries and white, and that the pigments both reflect and absorb light, so a color that is too bright can be altered by adding its complementary (or its light absorber), you can calculate the mixing of colors quite accurately. Black, as we have seen, is a total light absorber and is much more powerful than any other color, so it not only cancels out the complementary but makes the whole mix duller and less reflective, and should be avoided when mixing color.

This method of color mixing relies on the absorption and reflection of light and leads to a fairly subdued use of color, because the pigments ultimately all mix together to produce black, absorbing the light that hits them. This is known as **subtractive mixing**. Another way of mixing colors is to place small dots of pure color next to each other, so that the individual colors remain as bright and as intense as possible but, when seen from a distance, merge and reveal the image in color and tone. For instance, a pale blue sky could be made up of blue dots and white dots. A tree in front could be more blue dots and green dots, or it could be blue dots and yellow dots, which would then at a distance merge to become green.

This is known as **additive mixing** and painting in this manner operates in two ways. Firstly, it produces a more luminous effect, because it works by mixing the reflected light rather than reflecting the mixed pigment. Instead of tending toward black, as does subtractive mixing, additive mixing

ABOVE
Kimm Stevens
Barge with Tree
Pastel, 21 × 30 inches (54 × 77 cm)
By linking the near barge and the distant tree, the surface of the picture dominates and one is aware of the shape before the object. The cold green finally forces the tree into the background.

RIGHT AND ABOVE RIGHT
Kimm Stevens
River Wey
Pastel, 22 × 30 inches (57 × 77 cm)
This series shows the combined use of watercolor sketch and photograph to produce a studio pastel. The watercolor is essential in conveying the essence of the scene, the photograph provides the facts of proportion and captures the shafts of sunlight between the trees. These are then combined in the studio to produce the final piece, which concentrates on achieving luminosity and light through harmonies between warm and cool blues, greens and grays.

tends toward white because all the colors of the light spectrum mix together to produce white light. Secondly, it allows the painting to relate to itself across the whole surface. A blue dot in the sky will relate visually to a similar blue which is part of a tree. The sky may be made gray by adding complementary oranges and reds which, in turn, may relate to the reds of buildings or pathways. Thus the eye can be led across the surface of the painting, without any one element becoming separated from the whole image. This method of painting was exploited in the landscape by the Impressionists, and especially by Camille Pissarro, who often painted with firm dashes of color right across the canvas, filling shadows with blues and reds and linking sky and land with blues, greens and whites. It was developed and formulated by Georges Seurat into the technique

ABOVE LEFT
Barge photograph.

ABOVE RIGHT
Barge sketch.

Bushy Park   G. Crawford 93©

Bushy Park   G. Crawford © 93.

Bushy Park   G. Crawford 93©

known as the Divisionist, and later the Pointillist, style of painting.

The third method of color mixing is by the use of **glazes**. This is of paramount importance in watercolor painting, but is also useful in acrylic and oil painting. A glaze is basically a thin transparent layer of pigment, which allows the color of the surface underneath to show through. In watercolor painting, the white paper is often used as the light source and tones are established by laying in carefully planned areas of color, which themselves maintain a luminosity by being thin enough for the white still to shine through. Different colors can be achieved by glazing one pure color over another; for instance, one green can be made by laying yellow over blue, a different green by laying blue over yellow! A glaze of red over its complementary, green, will produce brown or darker tones. Colors can be cooled down or warmed up by delicate applications of blues or reds. Warm or cool versions of primary colors will produce very different secondary colors. Glazing is an extremely subtle and delightful way of painting, but requires disciplined decisions based on drawing to prevent the subject from becoming vague and woolly.

In oil painting, glazes are prepared by mixing paint with linseed oil and a little turpentine, which thins the color down but retains a certain amount of body to the paint. Glazes should be applied by a soft brush with the painting laid flat, and must be allowed to dry before further layers are applied. Glazing was used extensively in oil painting up until the mid-nineteenth century, when the Impressionists abandoned it in favor of a more direct application of color. Glazing offers many delicate and subtle effects, however, and the method should be explored and exploited. A very practical use of an oil glaze, to help revitalize a painting, is to rub into the dry painting a thin glaze of Prussian Blue. This reduces the color and heightens the tones, which reinforces the basic form and structure of the picture. The painting can then continue working into the wet glaze, which has a gentle, softening effect on the paint.

Color is a ludicrously complex issue in painting. I have tried to explain some basic theories and their direct practical use. I have not touched on the equally important emotional or symbolic uses of color, because an objective approach is initially more appropriate in landscape painting, and provides a basis from which to develop interpretation and expression.

George Crawford
Landscape painting series
Acrylic on paper
This series of paintings was made over a period of ten weeks by one of my students. It lucidly demonstrates a growing understanding of the dynamics that exist between color and tone. The first painting (far left top) is predominantly green, but there is little evidence of the light source and its effect on form and color. This results in a fairly flat image. As the series develops, the student becomes more confident with color and experiments with extending the range of green into blues and yellows; the tone and color relationships become more dynamic and the sense of space and volume is enhanced. By the final painting (above), the landscape is depicted almost entirely through color. Separate areas of the landscape, e.g. blue sky, green land, are now integrated, as the eye relates blues in the shadows to blues in the sky, reds in the branches to pinks in the sky, thus consolidating both the picture surface and the illusion.

5. Composition

Composition embraces all the techniques and theories of painting that we have discussed, and brings them to life. It is the very basis of expression and the vehicle through which the artist conveys his or her ideas. At its most basic level, composition is the arrangement of shapes and lines on a surface which makes up the picture. In terms of landscape it is where key elements, like the horizon, trees and buildings, are placed on the canvas to make an arrangement.

How various elements are placed on the canvas is surprisingly important, because we are dealing with a two-dimensional illusion of space. Things which in real life we can accept as being distant from each other suddenly develop very powerful visual relationships when translated into two dimensions. A classic example of this is the wedding photograph, where the photographer fails to take into account the background and the bridegroom has a telegraph pole sticking out of the top of his head. Now this inadvertent 'mistake' illustrates a fundamental property of painting and composition: that, while dealing with an illusion of the three-dimensional world, we are in fact working upon a flat surface which has its own geometry and sets up its own relationships beyond mere illusion. Perhaps the

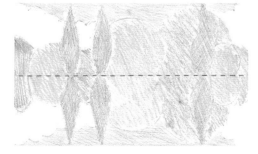

LEFT
Joe McGillivray
Birkenhead Docks II
Mixed media, 43 × 63 inches (110 × 161 cm)
Here realism is secondary to the pattern and weight offered by the shapes inherent in an industrial landscape.

TOP RIGHT
The position of the vertical axis helps define space: centrally it emphasizes symmetry and flatness; placed to the left or right it creates a feeling of space and movement, the eye being given a contrast of size in the division of the basic rectangle.

BELOW FAR LEFT
Symmetry. Vertically the image appears flat; horizontally it can be read as a reflected landscape.

BELOW
The different horizon heights create a different feeling of space; the space is symmetrically even (far left); the large sky appears very spacious (center); the land dominates and creates a more oppressive feeling (below).

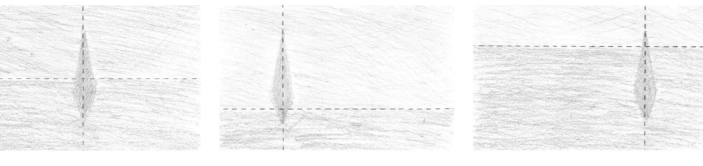

classic mistake dreaded by wedding photographers is, ironically, the key to the true excitement and power that is inherent in composition. We must always be aware of the flat relationships between shapes across the canvas as we build the illusion of space.

Dividing the Picture Surface

Within composition, there are various possible basic divisions of the canvas. There is the very powerful device of symmetry, which tends to flatten and emphasize the two-dimensional surface and is used for decorative effects. In landscape it exists in reflections and is useful for linking one area to another. Dividing the canvas evenly, with a horizontal and vertical line, will emphasize flatness. Taking the horizontal line as a horizon, and placing it higher or lower than the center, creates a different feeling and begins to suggest an implication of space. Placing the vertical axis off-center increases this sense of space. Because the horizontal and vertical axes are parallel to the sides of the rectangle, they are always closely related to it and tend to emphasize flatness. If we introduce a more contrasting diagonal, the illusion of space becomes more powerful, because of the contrasting dynamic and the implied possibility of perspective. Separating some lines from the edges and corners of the canvas further strengthens this illusion.

Square of the Rectangle

The rectangle of the canvas itself plays an important role; your eye and brain are constantly comparing the shorter dimension to

the longer, so a relationship can be developed and emphasized along the division created by the shorter on the longer side, producing a powerful position within the canvas. This is known as the square of the rectangle and can be projected from both sides. If you find the squares of the rectangle in an Old Master painting, it is amazing how many crucial and important things occur on those lines.

Golden Section

Another very useful division of the painting to be aware of is the Golden Section. This is a harmonious division of a line, where the ratio between the longer section and the total length of the line is the same as that be-

ABOVE
Kimm Stevens
Day by the Sea
Oil on canvas, 36 × 48 inches (92 × 123 cm)
Changes in scale and a high viewpoint create emotional tension.

BELOW
Diagonals create much more active movement within a composition: placed centrally and symmetrically (far left) produces an effect of greater flatness; placed obliquely high or low, or to the left or right, produces movement and space.

tween the shorter section and the longer section. Because each length relates in some way to the other, a perpetual harmony and balance is obtained which is visually very satisfying. The golden section of a line can be found by following the simple steps illustrated. Once the line has been divided, the longer section can be projected vertically to construct a rectangle in the golden section. This adds to the glory of it all, because now the square of the rectangle is also on the golden section, which produces even more powerful relationships and coincidences. The remaining rectangle is itself, once again, in the golden section, which can be squared once more to produce an even smaller rectangle on the golden section. You can go on forever producing smaller and smaller harmonious divisions of the rectangle.

Now if you plot a diagonal through all the squares, you should obtain a spiral, a beautiful, organic, natural growth form, perhaps a clue as to why the golden section seems to us natural and organic, somehow 'right' and satisfying. When a painting feels 'right', it is often because these more mathematical divisions have been instinctively satisfied. So don't panic and construct everything in the golden section, but be aware of the possibil-

ities offered by these factors while you paint and, if the painting does not feel right, try positioning some important elements in the composition on these lines and see if things

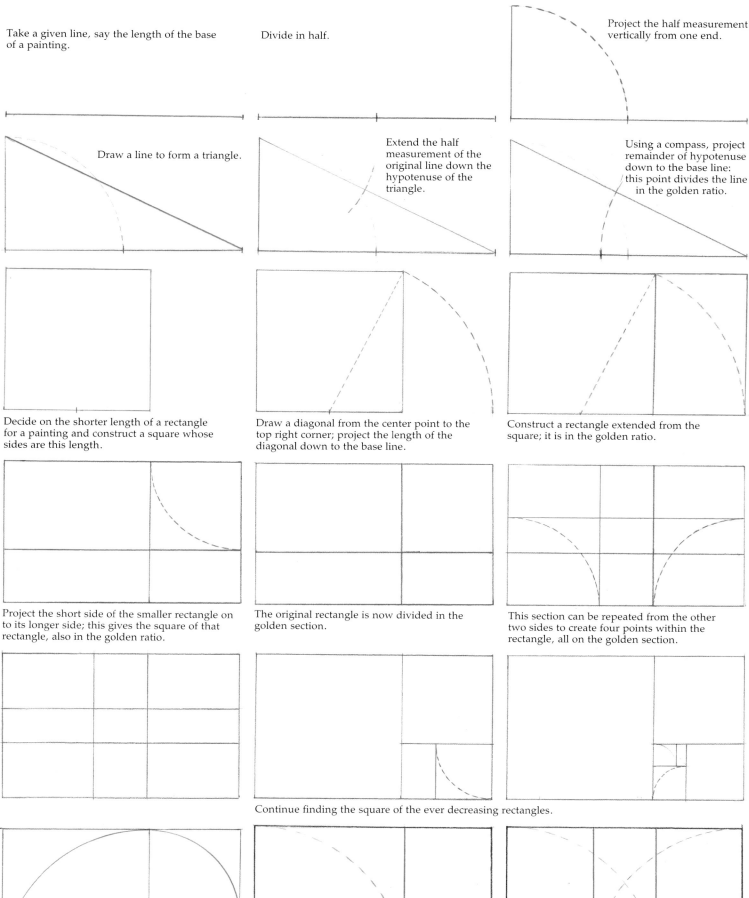

Take a given line, say the length of the base of a painting.

Divide in half.

Project the half measurement vertically from one end.

Draw a line to form a triangle.

Extend the half measurement of the original line down the hypotenuse of the triangle.

Using a compass, project remainder of hypotenuse down to the base line: this point divides the line in the golden ratio.

Decide on the shorter length of a rectangle for a painting and construct a square whose sides are this length.

Draw a diagonal from the center point to the top right corner; project the length of the diagonal down to the base line.

Construct a rectangle extended from the square; it is in the golden ratio.

Project the short side of the smaller rectangle on to its longer side; this gives the square of that rectangle, also in the golden ratio.

The original rectangle is now divided in the golden section.

This section can be repeated from the other two sides to create four points within the rectangle, all on the golden section.

Continue finding the square of the ever decreasing rectangles.

Drawing a curve, using the side of each diminishing square as a radius, produces a spiral.

Constructing the square of a rectangle by projecting the shorter onto the longer side.

This can be done from both sides.

start to fall into place. The golden section can be constructed from both sides, and obviously from the vertical as well as the horizontal sides, of the rectangle. Once again, it is extremely revealing to construct these lines on a postcard of an Old Master painting, just to see how much use is made of them.

So far we have divided the picture composition up with basic straight lines, which are very powerful because they relate directly to the edges of the canvas, help link one side visually with another, and project the composition right across the surface. They guide the eye across the picture and gently direct the viewer around the image in

the way that you, the artist, want. This gives you great power to create different moods and forms of expression, depending on how you devise your picture, which is really what composition is all about.

There are, however, many other ways to guide the eye around the picture. Lines that repeat are linked by the eye, so a row of poplar trees sets up a rhythmic pattern that the eye will respond to. Reflections of sky and trees in water again set up a visual link and rhythm. By establishing a visual rhythm, say of poplar trees, you can speed up or slow down the eye's journey across the picture space, by varying the intervals or spaces between the trees.

ABOVE
Peter Lloyd-Jones
Coombe Lake
Oil on board, 14 × 14 inches (36 × 36 cm)
The repeated rhythm of reflected trees carries the eye across the canvas.

ABOVE RIGHT
Ginny Chalcraft
Wapping
Watercolor and colored pencil, 10¼ × 20 inches (26 × 51 cm)
Composition as a collage.

RIGHT
Geoff Humphries
Tree
Oil on board, 18 × 24 inches (46 × 61 cm)
Strong use of curves and circles.

If the eye is guided by graceful swirling curves, it travels in a more flowing way, producing a gentler, slower image. The position of the main elements of the image on the canvas is also very important. If they are placed toward the top of the canvas they have a potential energy; there is a suggestion that they may fall down the surface, they are in tension and are dynamic. If they are placed along the bottom of the image, they have landed and expended their energy and appear to be more tranquil.

This, in landscape painting, often relates to the level of the horizon. A low horizon allows for large expansive, spatial skies; a high horizon suggests land piling up into a claustrophobic density of overwhelming power and scale. If the image is cut by the sides of the canvas it appears to be dramatically close to the viewer, which creates a powerful sense of movement in the canvas. This device must be used with great care as the nearness produces a very dramatic change in scale, though it can be highly spectacular if used well.

Composition and Tone

These linear elements of composition operate in tone as well. For instance, a strong light source will emphasize form and give a constant directional movement across the image. Shadows automatically repeat their objects visually and, at the same time, they subtly distort them, depending on how the light source is placed. A strong positive light source is also very useful in maintaining an interesting level of contrast, that is an effective balance between dark areas and light areas. If there is too much light, the picture may appear bland; too much dark and it may appear dull. It is often a good idea to identify an area that is totally dark and one that is pure white, and operate the tonal range of the picture between these two extremes, thus ensuring you are using the total tonal range available to you.

One of the major tonal problems in landscape is that the composition can so easily fall into two halves, the light sky meeting the darker land. On occasion this simple relationship can be quite elegant, and the composition can exploit this fact as long as the division is carefully considered. There are, however, limitations to this form of composition, and a far richer approach is to find similarities of tone between the sky and the land, thus linking them visually.

Water is a very useful feature which re-flects the sky, thus bringing the tone of the sky down into the land. Similarly, clouds in the sky break the light and cast shadows, which may make the sky as dark as the lighter parts of the landscape, thus making it more complex and interesting, and linking it with the land. Vertical features such as buildings, trees and hills have a different tonality to the horizontal plain of the landscape, so can be used to cut across the horizon and link the tones of the sky and the land with a third tone.

ABOVE
Sally Dray
Iona
Oil, 40×20 inches (102×51 cm)
The segments of sky echo the landscape below.

RIGHT ABOVE
Kimm Stevens
Snow Barge
Pastel, 22×36 inches (56×92 cm)
Here the dimensions are in the golden ratio.

RIGHT
Joe McGillivray
Birkenhead Docks I
Oil, 48×60 inches (123×154 cm)

By carefully considering all these possibilities, composition ideas can be developed as
you paint the landscape. A painting
becomes a process of finding the best way to
show what you are looking at, in terms of
creating an interesting and flowing composition on the canvas. Thus cloud shapes
may echo darker tree shapes, both of which
have been reflected in a lake. Your eye is fed
simultaneously with reflections, echoed
shapes and contrasts, which combine to
make a composition.

Composition and Color

Like tone, color plays an important role in
composition. We have seen how the eye responds to color, constantly linking similar
colors yet also relating complementaries to
each other. The tonal problem of the light
sky meeting the dark land can be resolved in
terms of color, by finding similar colors in
both land and sky and thus counteracting
the contrast through color, while allowing
the tonal difference to remain. So a yellow in
the sky will immediately relate to a yellow in
the land; they may be different tones and
temperatures, but they will still bridge the
divide ceated by the tonal difference.

Making use of complementaries is also an
important compositional idea. A neutral-

colored road or track running through green
fields will take on the complementary, red.
Make use of the contrast, maybe exaggerate
it a little, to create a color dynamic in the
composition. Trees that cut vertically across
the sky and the land can change color radic-
ally as their relationships to the sky and the

ABOVE
Jim Lee
House in Cornwall
Oil on board, 12 × 11 inches
(31 × 28 cm)
A very high horizon gives
space and energy to the
distant focal point of the
bright house.

LEFT
Kimm Stevens
In Suburbia
Oil on canvas, 48 × 60
inches (123 × 154 cm)
Taking an unusual
viewpoint, and simplifying
basic elements that make
up the artist's local
landscape, enables the
painting to convey
messages and images
beyond the objective.

RIGHT
Kimm Stevens
Backyard with Flying Panda
Charcoal, 30 × 22 inches
(77 × 56 cm)

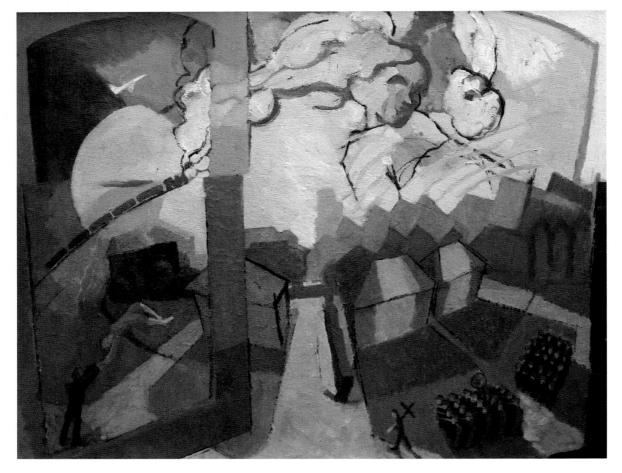

ABOVE
Kimm Stevens
The Garden
Oil on canvas, 30 × 40
inches (77 × 102 cm)
By taking a low viewpoint,
the artist creates a feeling of
tension and menace, which
is exacerbated by the long
shadows cast by the house
and children.

LEFT
Conor McFeely
Donegal
Oil on board, 36 × 42
inches (92 × 107 cm)
Both of McFeely's paintings
(see also page 70) show
radical use of paint and
color to express the feeling
of the landscape, rather
than to represent it. Much
control is needed, however,
to convey the image
through such an expressive
method.

Graham Rust's
Needlepoint Designs

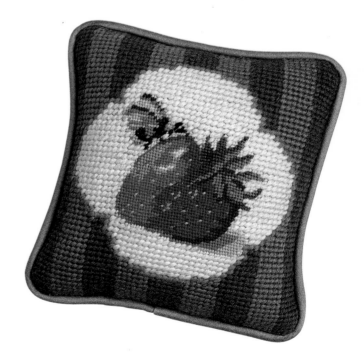

Graham Rust's
Needlepoint Designs

Over 20 Original Patterns, from Pincushion to Seashell Rug

Harry N. Abrams, Inc., Publishers

For Harry N. Abrams, Inc.:
Needlepoint consultant Karyn Gerhard

Library of Congress Cataloging-in-Publication Data

Rust, Graham.
Graham Rust needlepoint designs : over 20 original patterns
from pincushion to seashell rug / by Graham Rust ;
photographs by Shona Wood.
p.   cm.
ISBN 0–8109–3783–2 (hardcover)
1. Canvas embroidery—Patterns.   I. Title.
TT778.C3R895   1998
746.44'2—dc21   98–20308

Conceived and produced by Breslich & Foss Ltd, London

Printed and bound in Belgium

Harry N. Abrams, Inc.
100 Fifth Avenue
New York, N.Y. 10011
www.abramsbooks.com

CONTENTS

For my sisters Janet and Bridget

INTRODUCTION

A few years ago, my publishers asked me to produce a collection of decorative designs for the whole house. These included ideas for objects large and small, from firescreens to paperweights. Among the objects created for the book was a cushion featuring my French bulldog Bella. I had chosen Bella as she was very dear to me and a favourite subject for many years until she died in 1986 aged fifteen.

I decided to depict her in a rococo cartouche, and chose typical rococo elements – pearls, flowers and seashells – for the surrounding field.

The design was originally intended to be painted on silk, but for the book it was decided to interpret the pattern for needlepoint. Little did we know what a challenge we were setting the needleworkers.

My sketch was firstly copied directly onto the canvas. Then yarns were chosen that would exactly match the colours of the original watercolour. As a result, ninety-eight colours are used in the design; the background yellow alone accounts for five of these. Once the colours had been selected, it took two expert needleworkers the equivalent of five months' full-time sewing to complete the cushion.

One thing that I realised as the Bella cushion was being sewn, was that one cannot force the medium: large, straight stitches don't make delicate curves. This was something that I tried to bear in mind when selecting subjects for *Needlepoint Designs*. These are representative of some of the things that I like to paint, although the paintings had to be much simpler in many cases in order to work as tapestries.

As well as designs for several cushions, I have included patterns for a range of projects, such as evening bags, a tea cosy, a footstool and, perhaps slightly more unusual, a smoking cap.

I do hope that these tapestries will spark your interest and inspire you to create your own needlepoint designs or adapt and vary the patterns in this book.

Graham Hurst

Bella, the cartouche that surrounds her, the trellis and all the details – including my crest, a peacock butterfly – are sewn in petit point

the Designs

CABBAGE CUSHION

Canvas: 12-gauge single-thread canvas
49 × 53 cm (19½ × 21 in)
Tapestry needle size: 18
Approximate finished size:
34 × 38 cm (13½ × 15 in)
Embroidery threads: Appleton tapestry wool

Other materials: Ruler or tape measure
Masking tape • Scissors • Thimble • Pencil
Backing fabric • Matching thread
Cushion pad • Zipper (optional)
Cord furnishing trim (optional)

I have always liked the shape and form of the cabbage, and have drawn and painted it for many years. Its monochromatic quality also makes it a challenging subject for a needlepoint design. For this cushion I have kept the background deliberately simple, and have introduced little dots of green to add movement. A border worked in the same colour frames the cabbage and holds the design together.

STITCHING THE DESIGN

The design is 180 stitches wide by 162 stitches high. Work the design in tent stitch, following the chart and using one strand of tapestry wool. When working the background and border, add 16 more horizontal rows of background and 10 rows of pale green border across the bottom of the design, and 13 more rows of background and 6 rows of border across the top. Block the completed canvas and finish the cushion as explained in "Finishing techniques".

APPLETON COLOURS USED

- 741 pale blue (3 skeins)
- • 742 light blue (3 skeins)
- − 743 light medium blue (3 skeins)
- < 744 medium blue (3 skeins)
- 746 dark medium blue (4 skeins)
- ▼ 747 dark blue (2 skeins)
- ● 748 deep blue (1 skein)
- ✚ 934 dark mauve (1 skein)
- ✕ 935 deep mauve (1 skein)
- ☐ 146 dark rose (1 skein)
- S 952 light brown (1 skein)
- 4 761 beige (1 skein)
- 871 oatmeal (18 skeins)
- 331A pale green (7 skeins)

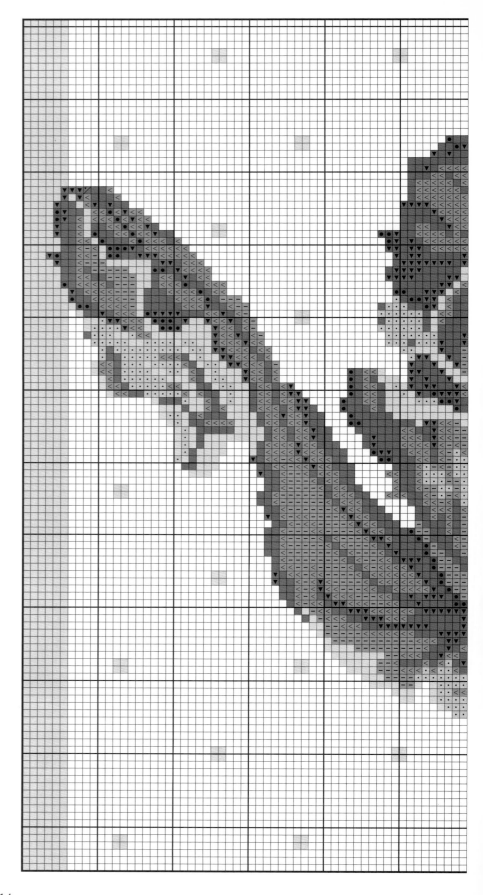

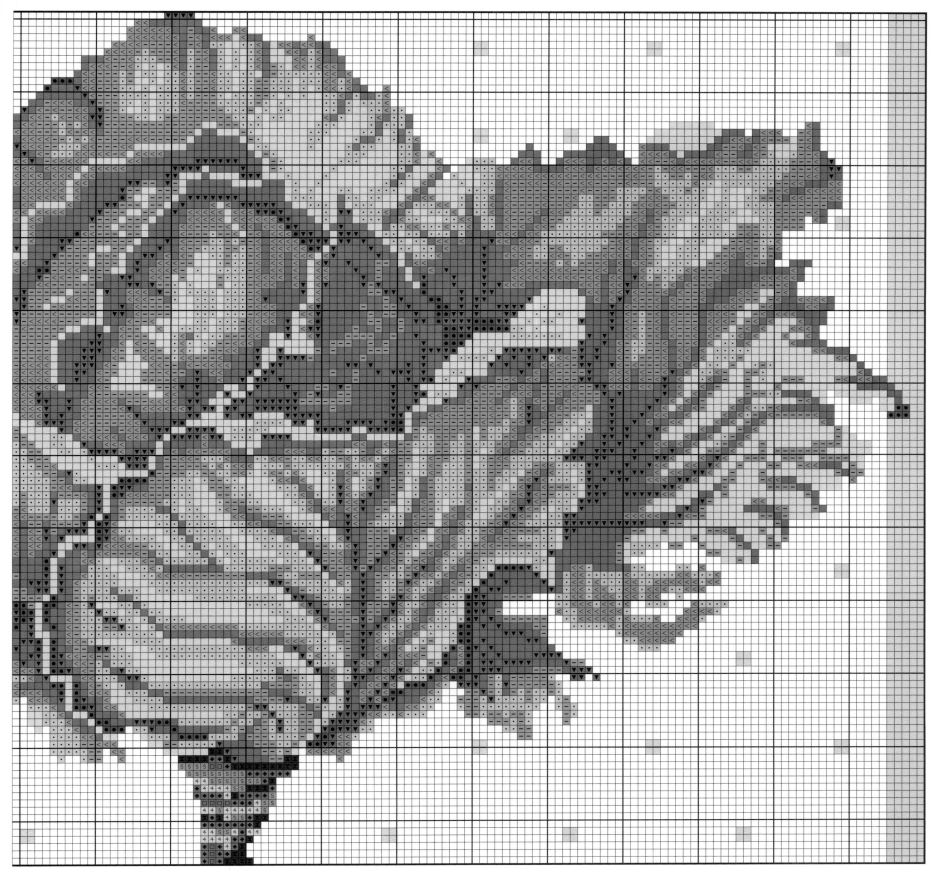

INSECTS GLASSES CASE

I enjoy drawing and painting insects and often use them in my mural work. For this needlepoint pattern I have enlarged the insects, as spindly legs and antennae are difficult to interpret in stitches. However, the butterfly, caterpillar and other creatures are kept in proportion to each other. I have found that it is generally easier to work from paintings and engravings of insects than photographs.

Canvas: 10-gauge double-thread canvas, two pieces each 23 × 32 cm (9 × 13 in)
Tapestry needle sizes: 22 and 18
Approximate finished size:
7.5 × 17 cm (3 × 6¾ in)
Embroidery threads:
DMC Médicis crewel wool

Other materials:
Ruler or tape measure • Masking tape
Scissors • Thimble • Pencil • Lining fabric
Matching thread

Green, the colour of summer leaves, throws the insects into relief

STITCHING THE DESIGN

The design is worked in both *gros point* and *petit point*. First, stitch the insects in *petit point* on one of the pieces of canvas, following one of the charts and using two strands of crewel wool. To work *petit point*, split the double-thread canvas and work each tent stitch over a single canvas thread (20 stitches per inch/2.5 cm).

When the *petit point* is complete, fill in the background in *gros point*, using four strands of crewel wool and working each tent stitch over a double-thread intersection (10 stitches per inch/2.5 cm). (Note that for the *gros point*, four chart squares equal a single stitch.) When the background *gros point* is complete, fill in the remaining *petit point* around the insects using the background colour. Work from the second chart in the same way.

Block the completed canvas and finish the glasses case as explained at the back of the book in "Finishing techniques".

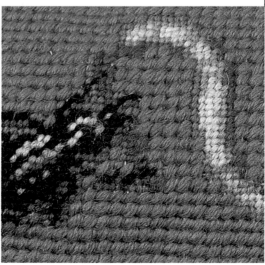

DMC COLOURS USED

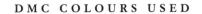

■	noir	black (1 skein)
▲	8500	charcoal (1 skein)
⊡	8713	dark grey (1 skein)
○	8507	medium grey (1 skein)
\	8508	light grey (1 skein)
+	8307	medium brown (1 skein)
▽	8422	dark khaki (1 skein)
=	8400	light khaki (1 skein)
	8406	sage green (9 skeins)
<	8503	light brown (1 skein)
Z	8313	gold (1 skein)
I	8027	lemon (1 skein)
◆	8126	dark red (1 skein)
	8666	medium red (1 skein)
T	8104	dark brick (1 skein)
⌐	8176	medium brick (1 skein)
N	8166	light brick (1 skein)
	8118	pale pink (1 skein)
□	ecru	off-white (1 skein)

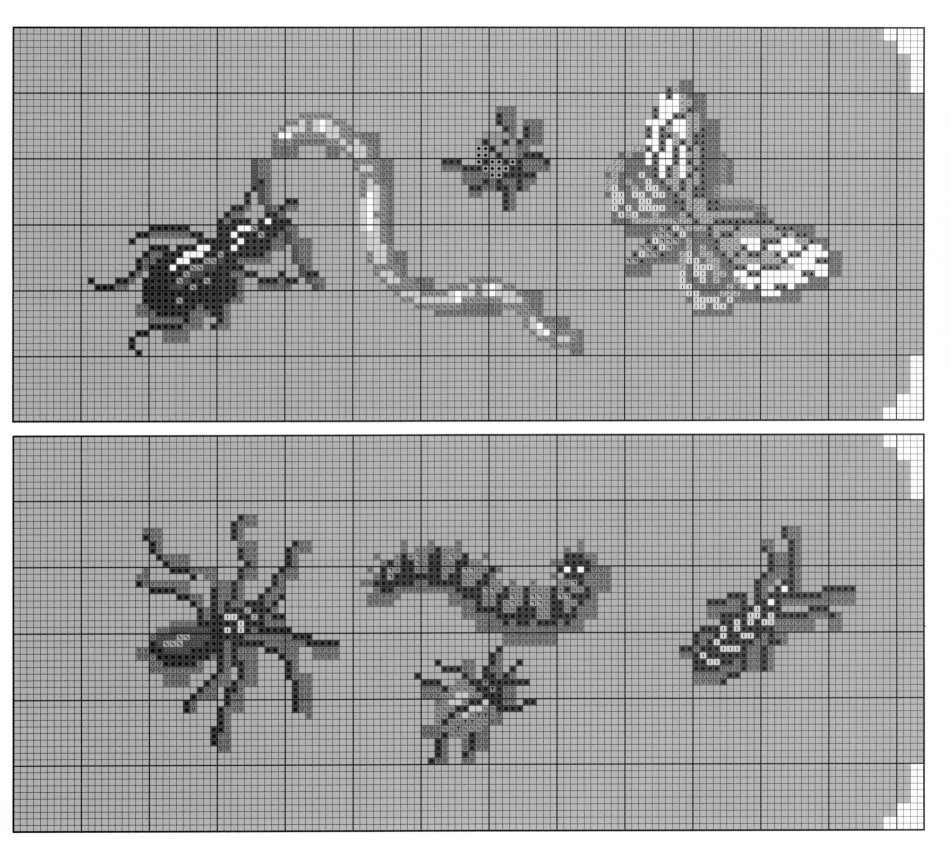

ROSA MUNDI CUSHION

I chose Rosa mundi *for a needlepoint design because I particularly like the striped petals of this old rose. The original sketch was painted from life, as are all my flower studies. The background to the design is a trellis pattern, which echoes the garden, and I have added falling petals and a bee to lend movement to the piece.*

Canvas: 10-gauge double-thread canvas
70 × 70 cm (28 × 28 in)
Tapestry needle size: 18
Approximate finished size:
53 × 55 cm (21 × 21½ in)
Embroidery threads: Anchor tapestry wool

Other materials: Ruler or tape measure
Masking tape • Scissors • Thimble
Pencil • Backing fabric • Matching thread
Cushion pad • Zipper (optional)
Cord furnishing trim (optional)

STITCHING THE DESIGN

The design is 209 stitches wide by 215 stitches high. Work the design in tent stitch, following the chart and using one strand of tapestry wool. Work the rose and leaves first, then fill in the background. Work the border last. Block the completed canvas and finish the cushion as explained in "Finishing Techniques".

Turn to page 24 for the yarn key.

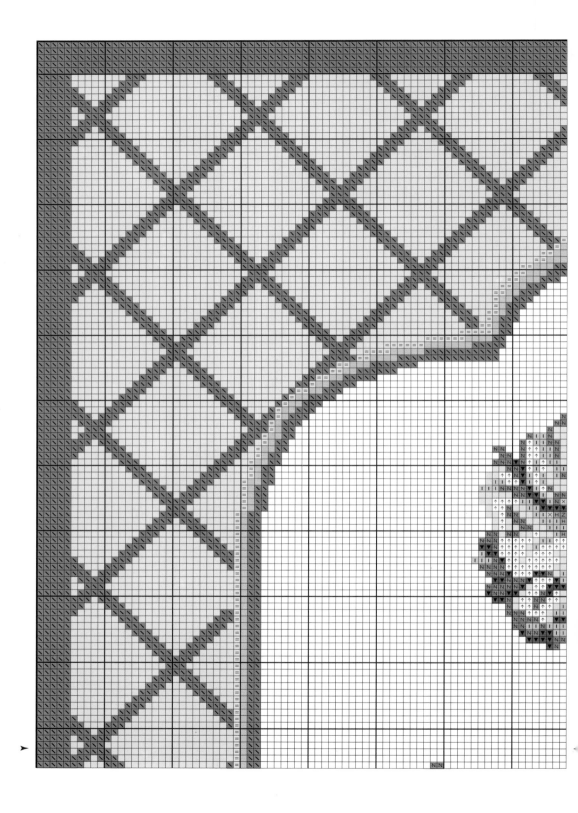

ANCHOR COLOURS USED

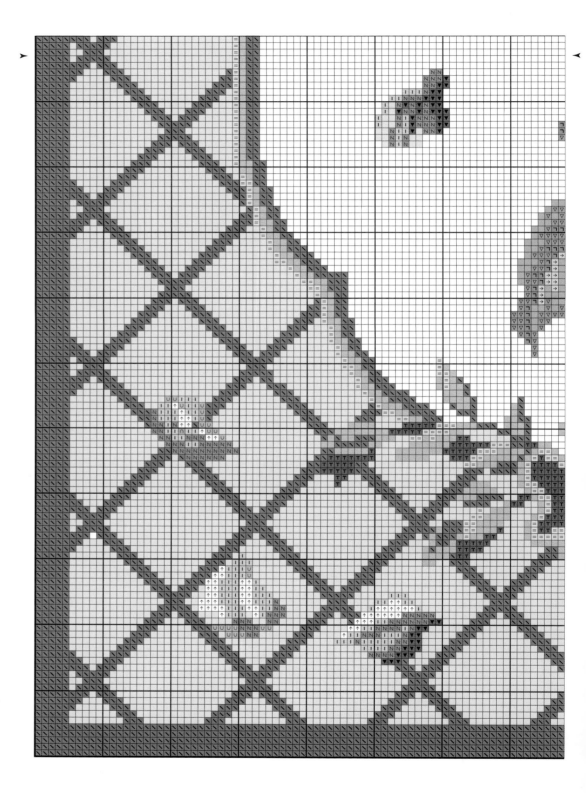	8900	medium sea green (17 skeins)
	8704	pastel grey blue (26 skeins)
=	8814	pale blue (2 skeins)
	8818	light blue (2 skeins)
↑	8000	white (1 skein)
U	9790	medium grey (1 skein)
	9800	black (1 skein)
◆	9796	dark grey (1 skein)
T	8880	dark grey green (1 skein)
	8004	off-white (20 skeins)
—	8412	pale raspberry (1 skein)
∩	8414	light raspberry (1 skein)
	8420	medium raspberry (1 skein)
⊡	8442	dark raspberry (1 skein)
→	9092	pastel green (1 skein)
	9162	light olive green (1 skein)
▽	9102	medium green (2 skeins)
⌐	9006	dark green (1 skein)
X	8054	light gold (1 skein)
H	8100	medium gold (1 skein)
Z	8102	dark gold (1 skein)
O	9404	light golden brown (1 skein)
●	8106	dark golden brown (1 skein)
I	8394	pale rose pink (1 skein)
N	8398	medium rose pink (1 skein)
▼	8400	dark rose pink (1 skein)

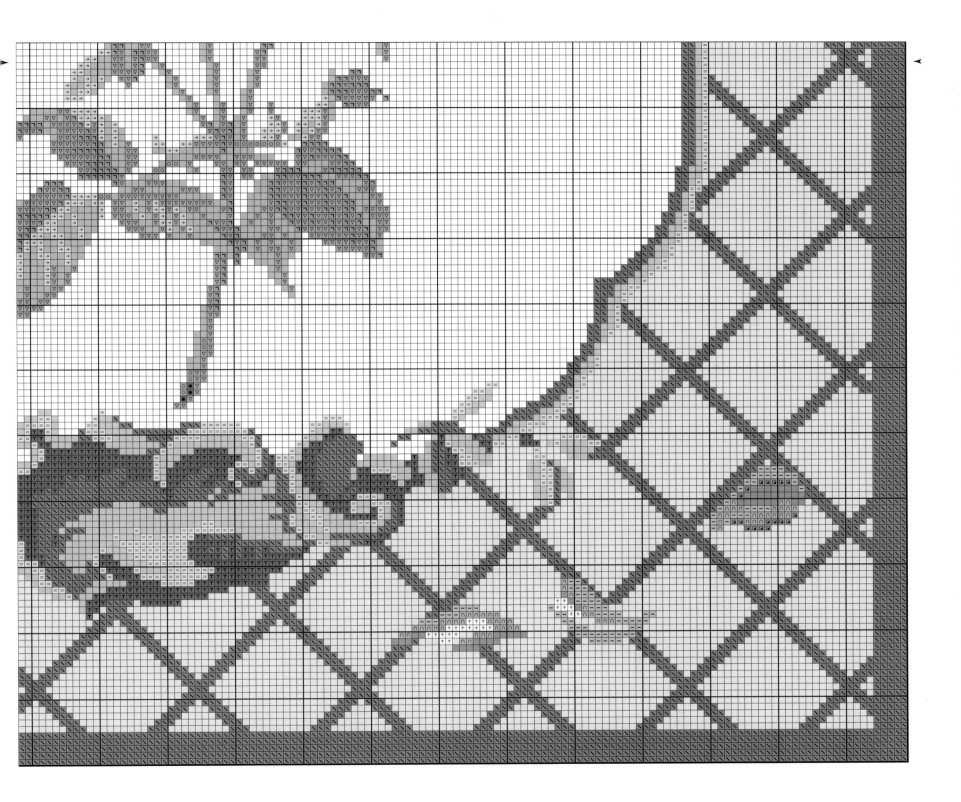

FROG PINCUSHION

A poison frog may seem an unusual choice for a needlepoint design, but the colour and size of this fellow make him the perfect subject for a pincushion. It is important to choose as a design something that is in proportion to the finished piece. Brightly coloured beetles and butterflies also make amusing subjects for small items, such as the glasses case project on page 16.

Canvas: 12-gauge double-thread canvas
25 × 25 cm (10 × 10 in)
Tapestry needle sizes: 24 and 18
Approximate finished size:
10 × 10 cm (4 × 4 in)
Embroidery threads:
Anchor stranded cotton

Other materials: Ruler or tape measure
Masking tape • Scissors • Thimble • Pencil
Backing fabric • Matching thread
Fabric for inner cushion • Pincushion
stuffing • Cord furnishing trim

Inspiration for needlepoint designs can be found in some unlikely places

STITCHING THE DESIGN

The design is worked in both *gros point* and *petit point*. First, stitch the frog in *petit point*, following the chart and using three strands of cotton thread. To work *petit point*, split the double-thread canvas and work each tent stitch over a single canvas thread (24 stitches per inch/2.5 cm).

When the *petit point* is complete, fill in the background in *gros point*, using 12 strands of cotton thread and working each tent stitch over a double-thread intersection (12 stitches per inch/2.5 cm). (Note that for the background, four chart squares equal a single stitch.) When the background *gros point* is complete, fill in the remaining *petit point* around the frog in the background colour. Then work the eye details in backstitch using a single strand of off-white thread.

Block the completed canvas and finish the pincushion as explained in "Finishing techniques".

ANCHOR COLOURS USED

●	149	deep blue (1 skein)
▲	979	dark blue (1 skein)
S	146	medium blue (1 skein)
	977	light medium blue (1 skein)
+	144	light blue (1 skein)
	128	pale blue (1 skein)
T	401	charcoal (1 skein)
▣	403	black (1 skein)
	926	off-white (1 skein)
	887	straw (3 skeins)

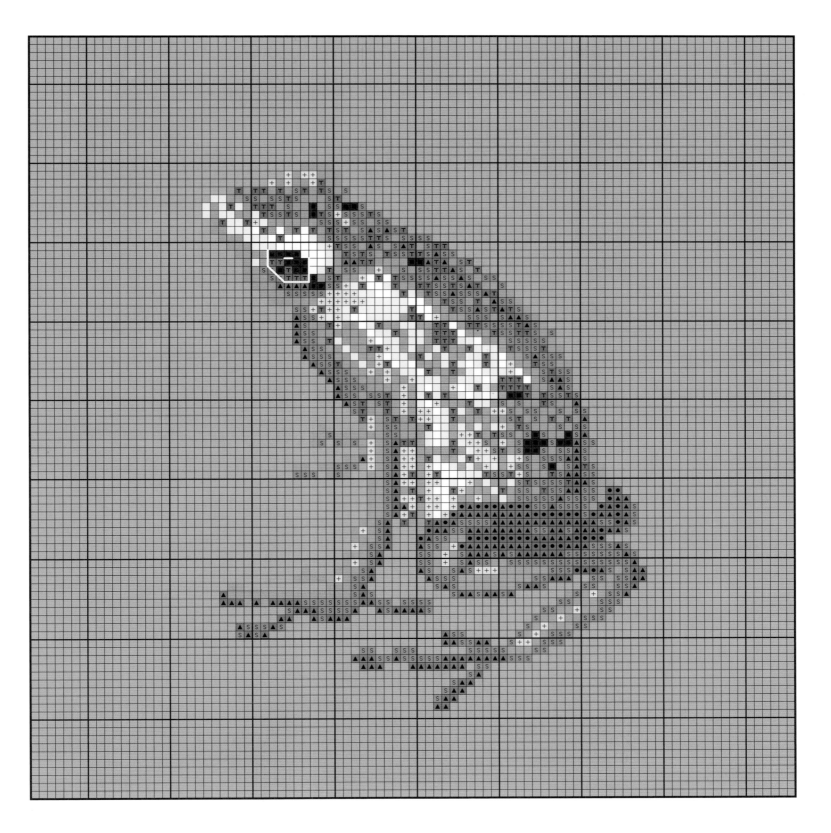

MOUSE AND TEAPOT TEA COSY

Canvas: 14-gauge single-thread canvas
51 × 51 cm (20 × 20 in)
Tapestry needle size: 20
Approximate finished size:
38 cm (14½ in) wide by
32 cm (12¾ in) high
Embroidery threads: Appleton crewel wool

Other materials: Ruler or tape measure
Masking tape • Scissors • Thimble
Pencil • Backing fabric • Matching thread
Cord furnishing trim
Lining fabric and padding

I was inspired to create this design for a tea cosy by the terracotta teapot. The face on the pot is a "grotesque" design, a style that was popular across Europe two centuries ago. As I have always loved Alice in Wonderland, *and particularly the Mad Hatter's tea party, the two elements have come together with, I hope, some amusement. The pattern can also be used for a cushion.*

In this design, I wanted to emphasise the dormouse, which is why I chose a teapot in a muted colour

STITCHING THE DESIGN

The design is 202 stitches wide by 178 stitches high. Work the design in tent stitch, following the chart and using two strands of crewel wool. Work the mouse and teapot first. Then for a tea cosy, fill in the background up to the bold curved line on the chart. To make a cushion, fill in the background to the edge of the chart.

Block the completed canvas and finish the tea cosy as explained in "Finishing techniques". See the Cabbage Cushion on page 12 for the Other Materials needed for a cushion, and "Finishing techniques" for instructions on how to make up a cushion cover.

Turn to page 34 for the yarn key.

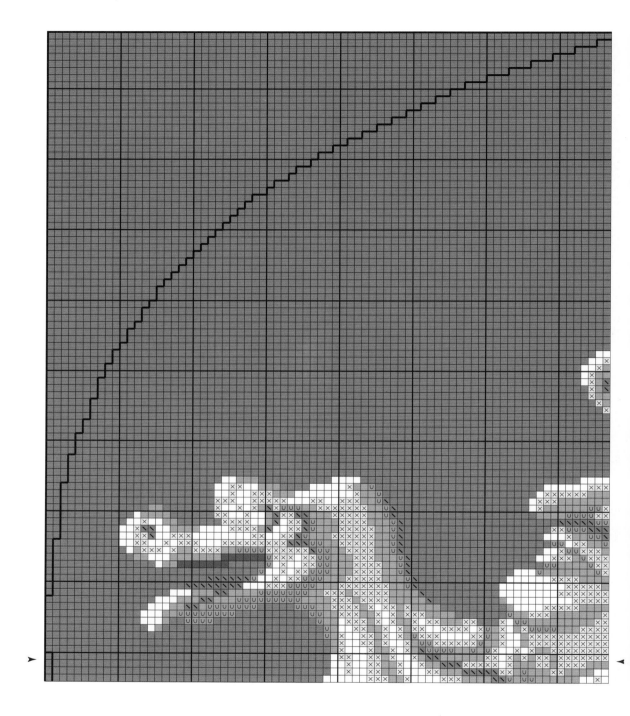

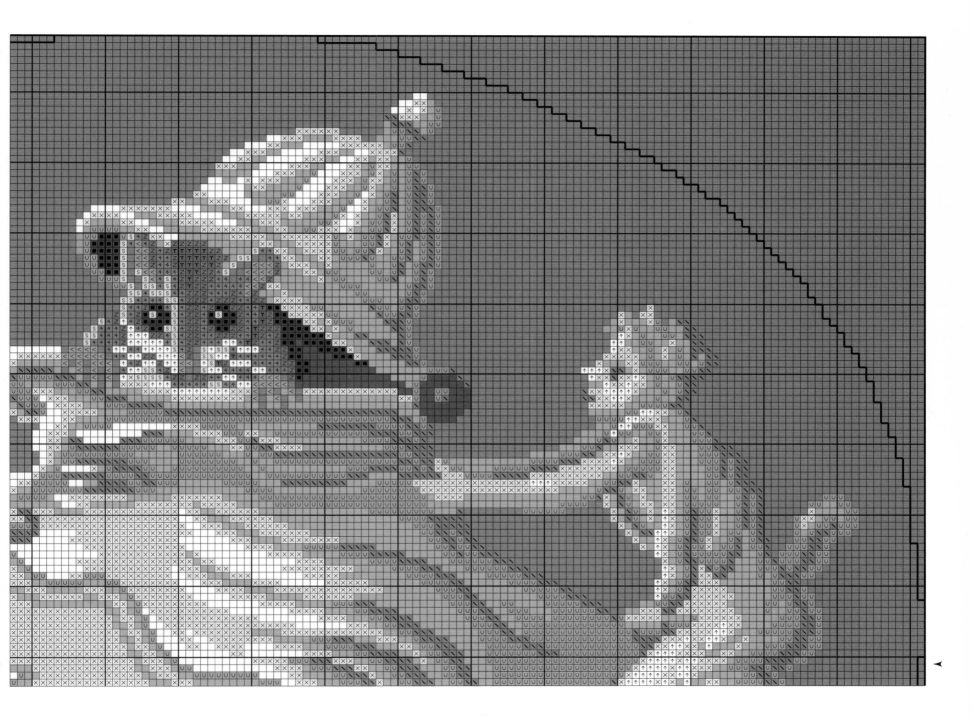

APPLETON COLOURS USED

	756	medium rose pink (18 skeins)
	754	light rose pink (1 skein)
	932	dark dusty rose (1 skein)
	142	light dusty rose (4 skeins)
	914	chocolate brown (1 skein)
	903	medium golden brown (3 skeins)
	901	light golden brown (4 skeins)
	761	light camel (4 skeins)
	181	pastel pink brown (3 skeins)
	991	off-white (1 skein)
	338	deep khaki brown (1 skein)
	336	dark khaki (1 skein)
	952	medium grey brown (1 skein)
	951	light grey brown (1 skein)
	989	pastel grey brown (1 skein)
	991B	white (1 skein)

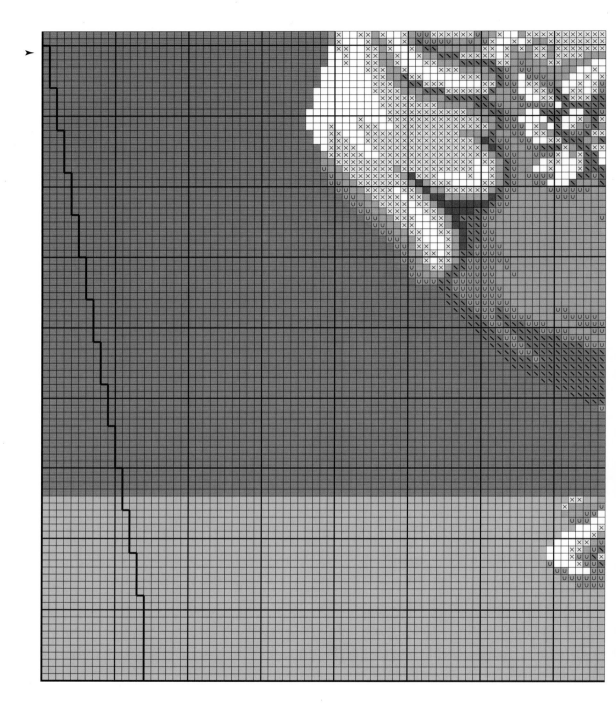

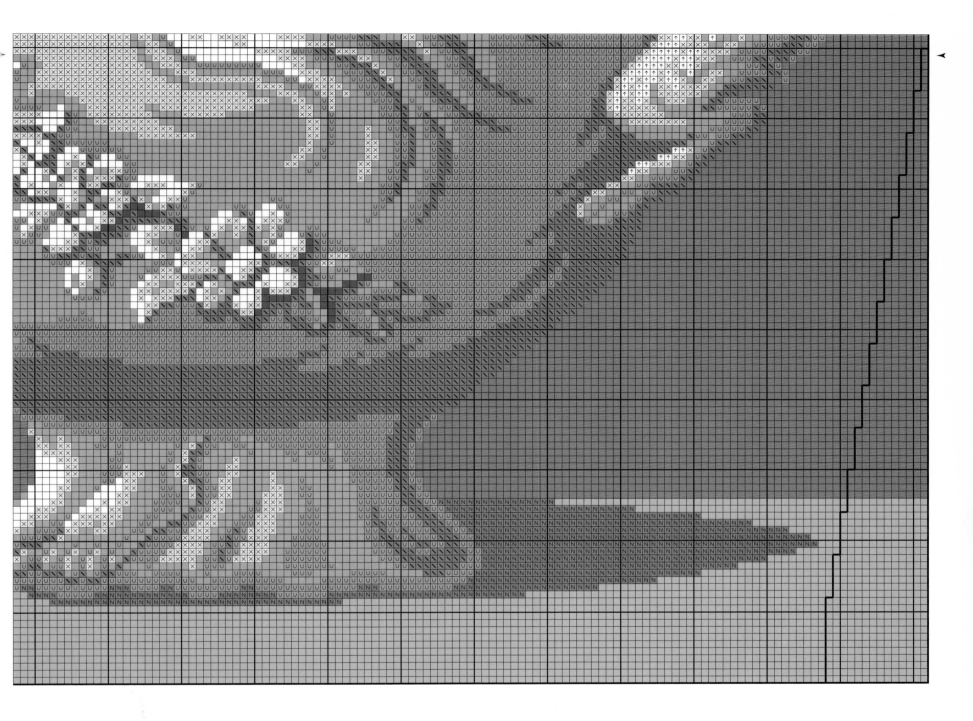

CHINESE VASES CUSHION

Canvas: 12-gauge single-thread canvas
50 × 50 cm (20 × 20 in)
Tapestry needle size: 18
Approximate finished size: 36 × 35 cm
(14¼ × 13¾ in)
Embroidery threads: Anchor tapestry wool

Other materials: Ruler or tape measure
Masking tape • Scissors • Thimble
Pencil • Backing fabric • Matching thread
Cushion pad • Zipper (optional)
Cord furnishing trim (optional)

Ginger jars, like the one worked here in needlepoint, were once filled with sweetmeats, ginger and tea and given as gifts at New Year. I found that the shapes and colours of these oriental vases worked very well together. As there is a clear relationship between the images and a tea pot, it would be fun to adapt the pattern as a tea cosy (see page 30).

STITCHING THE DESIGN

The design is 170 stitches wide by 165 stitches high. Work the design in tent stitch, following the chart and using one strand of tapestry wool. Work the pots first, then fill in the background. Block the completed canvas and finish the cushion as explained in "Finishing techniques". For the materials needed to make a tea cosy, see page 30. For instructions on making up the piece, turn to "Finishing techniques".

Turn to page 40 for the yarn key.

ANCHOR COLOURS USED

+	8016	yellow (1 skein)
	8018	light gold (7 skeins)
∩	8022	medium gold (1 skein)
⌐	8102	dark gold (1 skein)
	8114	lemon (8 skeins)
O	8686	pale blue (1 skein)
	8628	light blue (2 skeins)
X	8630	medium blue (2 skeins)
▼	8632	dark blue (1 skein)
	9800	black (1 skein)
S	9784	pastel grey (1 skein)
U	8714	pale grey blue (1 skein)
I	9790	light grey (2 skeins)
	8816	pale green blue (1 skein)
	8000	white (2 skeins)
	9056	pale moss green (4 skeins)
4	9062	light brown (1 skein)
\	9366	medium brown (1 skein)
T	9680	dark dusty rose (1 skein)
▽	9620	mid dusty rose (2 skeins)
	8262	medium brick (2 skeins)
●	8330	dark brick (1 skein)
	8366	light dusty rose (2 skeins)
	9772	pastel pink-grey (2 skeins)
<	9674	light beige pink (2 skeins)
N	8718	medium grey (1 skein)

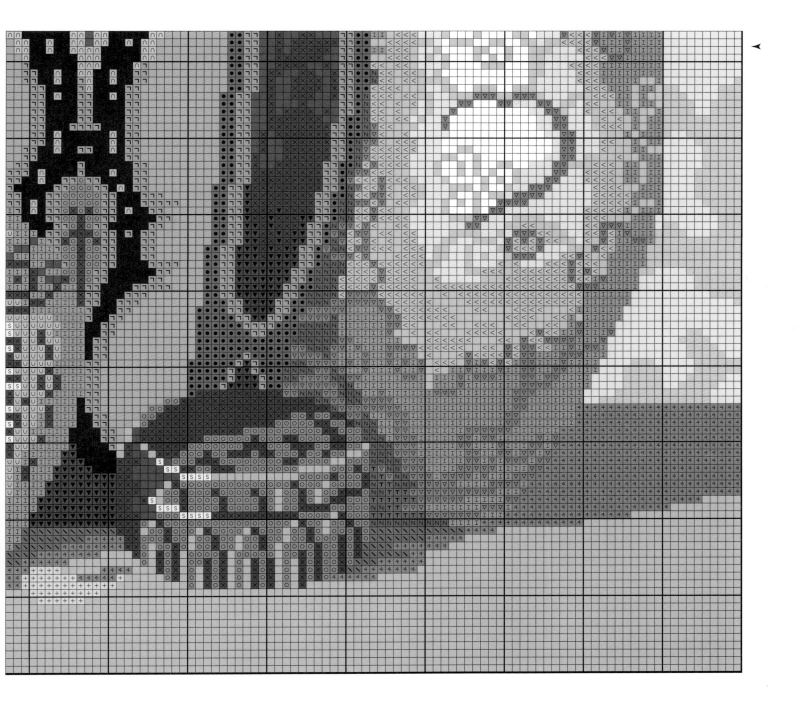

MONKEY CUSHION

In Europe in the seventeenth and eighteenth centuries, there was a vogue for decorating entire rooms with monkeys, both wild and dressed as humans. I enjoy painting monkeys and they feature in many of my murals. The image of a monkey playing "he loves me, he loves me not" was originally intended for a chimney board. For this cushion I have brightened the colours and added a trellis background, which I feel helps the oriental feel of the design.

Canvas: 10-gauge single-thread canvas
60 × 60 cm (24 × 24 in)
Tapestry needle size: 18
Approximate finished size: 44 × 45 cm
(17¼ × 17½ in)
Embroidery threads: Anchor tapestry wool

Other materials: Ruler or tape measure
Masking tape • Scissors • Thimble
Pencil • Backing fabric • Matching thread
Cushion pad • Zipper (optional)
Cord furnishing trim (optional)

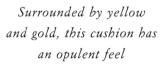

Surrounded by yellow and gold, this cushion has an opulent feel

STITCHING THE DESIGN

The design is 173 stitches wide by 175 stitches high. Work the design in tent stitch, following the chart and using one strand of tapestry wool. Work the monkey, cushion, flower and flower petals first, then work the trellis patterns. Fill in the background last. Block the completed canvas and finish the cushion as explained in "Finishing techniques".

ANCHOR COLOURS USED

—	8000	white (1 skein)
S	8704	pale grey (1 skein)
	8912	pale turquoise (12 skein)
	9074	light grey green (6 skeins)
↑	8014	light yellow (1 skein)
I	8044	gold (1 skein)
	9422	light camel (17 skeins)
O	9446	light nutmeg (1 skein)
↘	9448	mid nutmeg (1 skein)
	9256	light sage green (6 skeins)
↘	9260	dark sage green (1 skein)
◻	9314	dark khaki (1 skein)
	9102	bright green (1 skein)
L	9022	dark green (1 skein)

continued on page 46

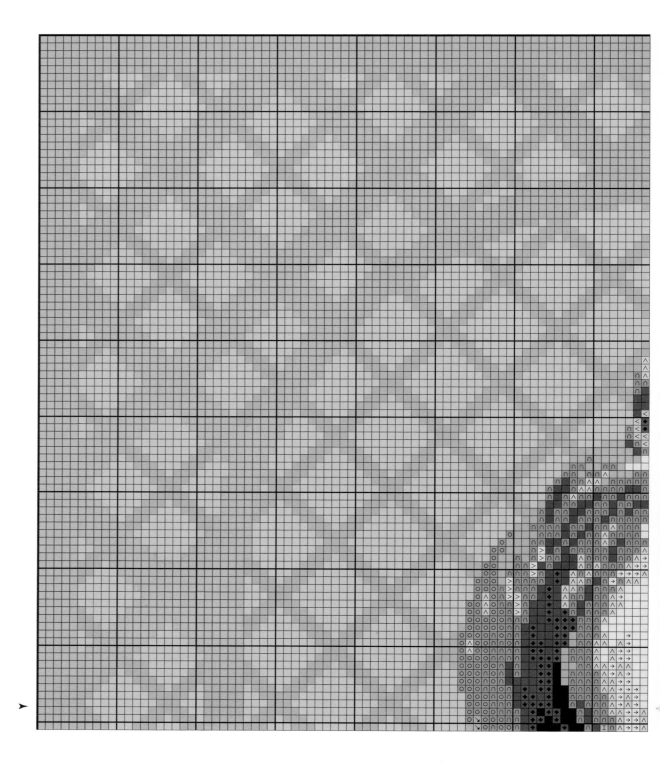

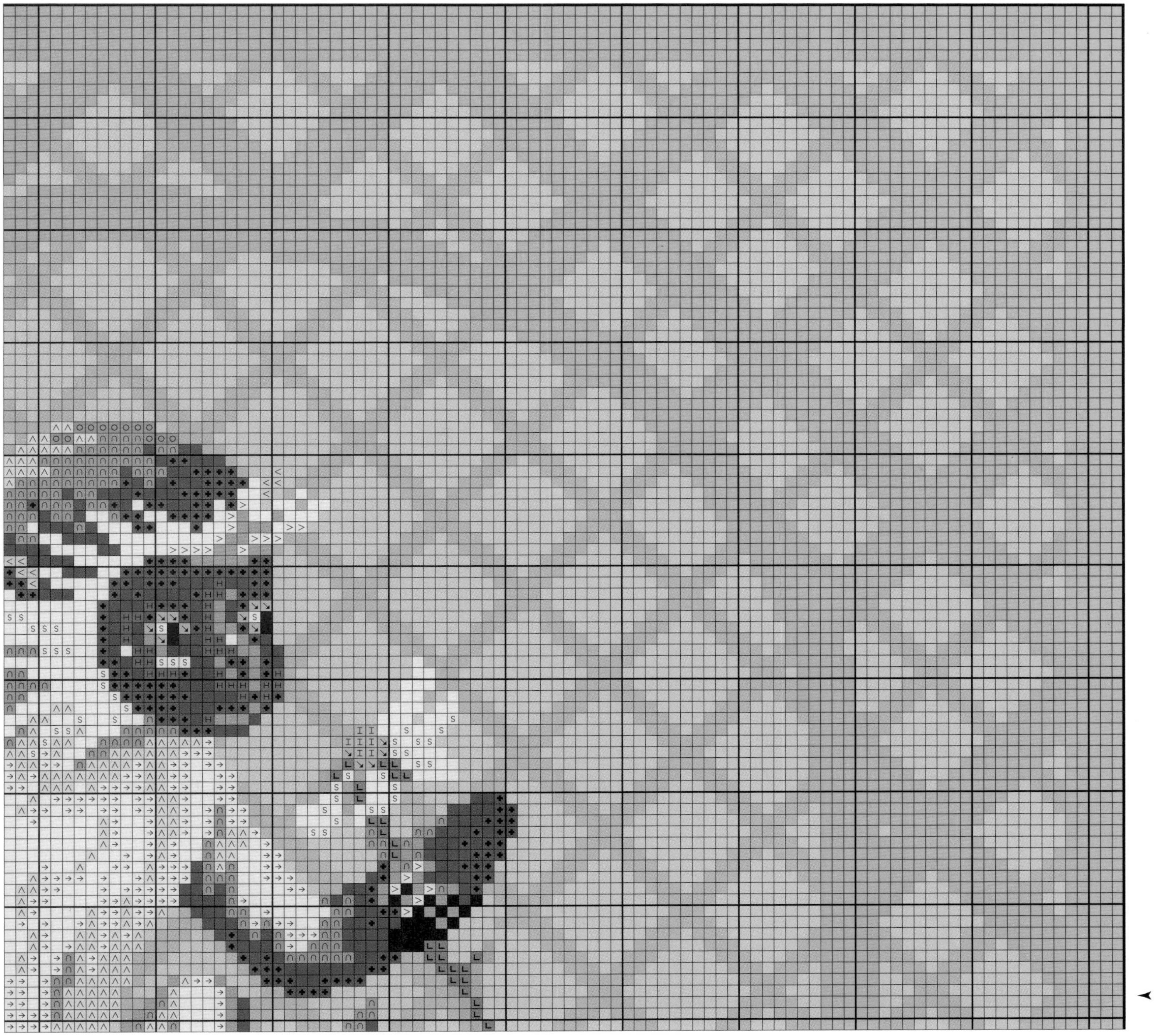

ANCHOR COLOURS USED

continued

	8006	off-white (1 skein)
>	9052	pale beige (1 skein)
→	252	pale sage green (1 skein)
∧	9056	light beige green (1 skein)
∩	9366	light brown (1 skein)
	9788	light grey (1 skein)
H	8718	medium steel grey (1 skein)
	9764	dark grey (2 skeins)
✚	9768	charcoal (1 skein)
	9800	black (1 skein)
<	8252	light terracotta (1 skein)
Z	8260	medium terracotta (1 skein)
	8240	medium red (1 skein)
●	8220	dark red (1 skein)

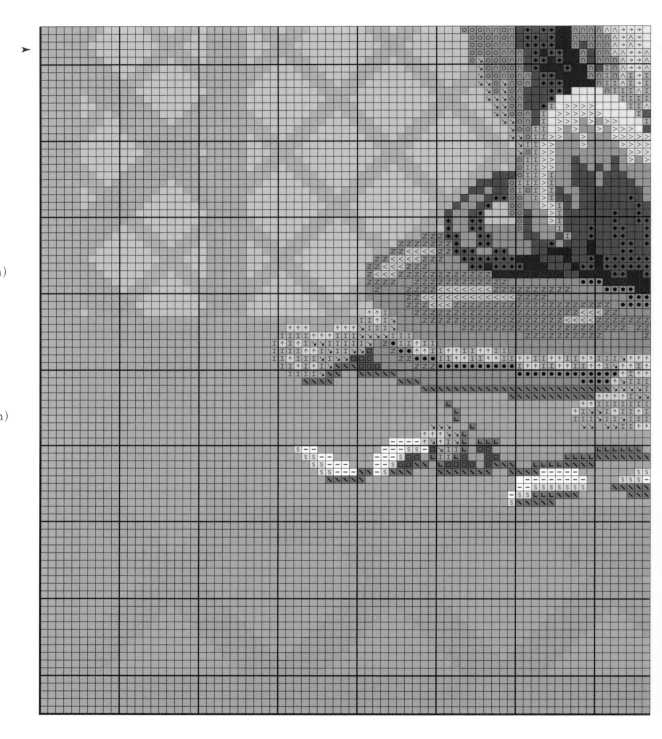

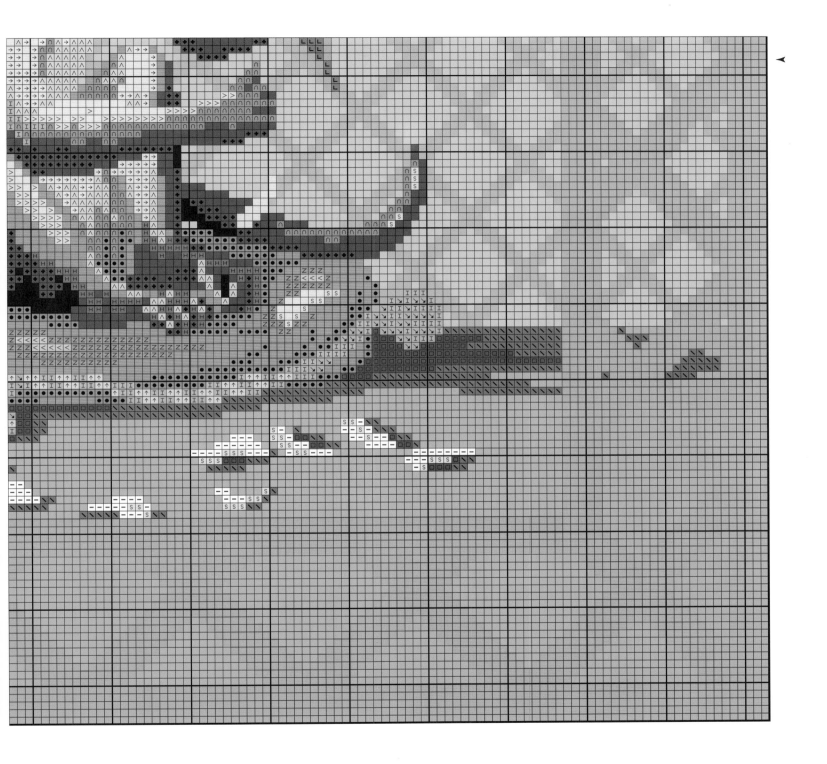

CHEETAH FOOTSTOOL

Cheetahs are magnificent animals, and I have had many requests to include them in my mural work. Paintings and engravings by other artists are generally the source of my animal studies; I have drawn live animals in zoos, but they are often unco-operative! For this simple design for a footstool or large cushion, I decided to place just the cheetah's head in a decorative frame on a blue background.

Canvas: 12-gauge single-thread canvas
58 × 58 cm (23 × 23 in)
or larger for a larger footstool
Tapestry needle size: 18
Approximate finished size:
42 × 43 cm (16½ × 17 in) or larger
for a larger footstool
Embroidery threads: Anchor tapestry wool

Other materials:
Ruler or tape measure • Masking tape
Scissors • Thimble • Pencil

STITCHING THE DESIGN

The charted design is 196 stitches wide
by 204 stitches high. If you intend to
make a cover for a footstool, obtain a
template from your upholsterer before
you begin the tapestry. If the extent of
the charted design is not big enough,
the border can be extended to fill
the correct area, but you may need to
purchase a larger piece of canvas and
more yarn. Trace the template shape
onto the canvas before stitching. For a
cushion, follow the chart and yarn
amounts given.

Work the design in tent stitch,
following the chart and using one strand
of tapestry wool. Work the cheetah
first, then work the border, repeating
the pattern to the template line for a
footstool cover and to the edge of the
chart for a cushion. Fill in the
background last.

For a footstool cover, block the
canvas to the size of the original
template, then have the needlepoint
stretched onto the footstool by your
upholsterer.

See the Cabbage Cushion on page
12 for the Other Materials needed for a
cushion, and "Finishing techniques"
for instructions on how to make up a
cushion cover.

Turn to page 52 for the yarn key.

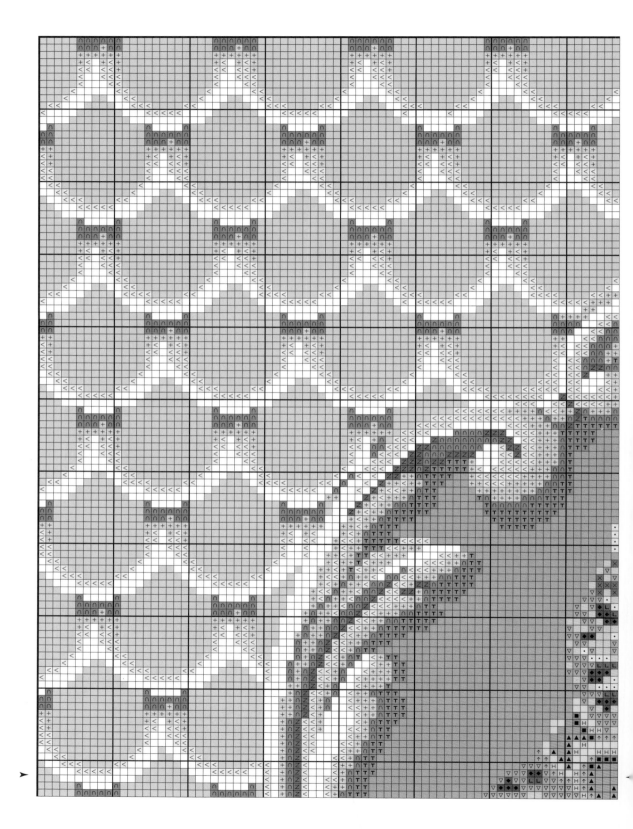

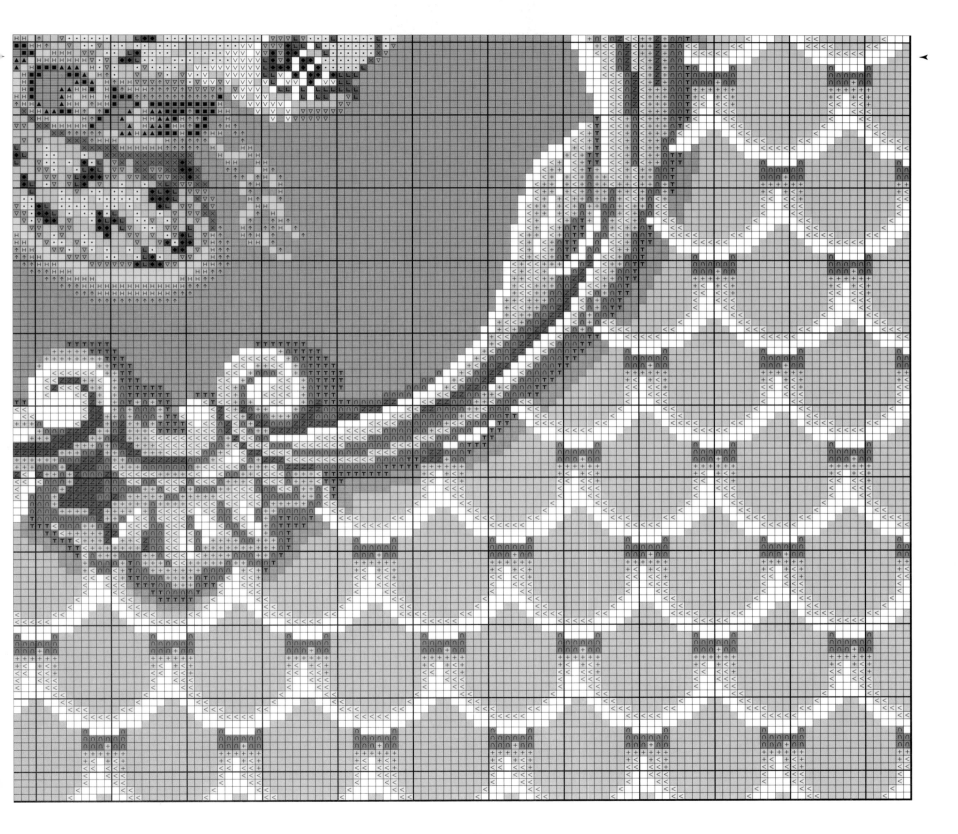

TORTOISE DOORSTOP

For this project, it was essential to choose as a subject something that one usually sees from above. It also had to be something that would be the right sort of size to sit on a brick. I had a tortoise as a child and was fascinated by the way it was constructed, but the pattern for the doorstop could equally well have been a mouse or a toad. The sides of the "brick" are decorated with grass and lichens. A brick doorstop is very useful, as it can easily be moved with one's foot, but a small cushion with a tortoise design is equally charming.

Canvas: 14-gauge single-thread canvas
54 × 41 cm (21 × 16 in)
Tapestry needle size: 20
Approximate finished size:
doorstop cover to fit brick approximately
24 × 11.5 × 6.5 cm (9½ × 4½ × 2½ in)
Embroidery threads: Appleton crewel wool

Other materials:
Ruler or tape measure • Masking tape
Scissors • Thimble • Pencil • Calico
Furnishing fabric • Matching thread

STITCHING THE DESIGN

The design is 204 stitches wide by 134 stitches high. Work the design in tent stitch, following the chart and using two strands of crewel wool. Work the tortoise first, then the border and the other details. Fill in the background last. Block the completed canvas and finish the doorstop as explained in "Finishing techniques".

To make a cushion, continue the border into the corners, then work extra medium olive green around the edge to increase the embroidered area to the desired size. Ensure that you buy a piece of canvas large enough for the cushion, plus 7.5 cm (3 in) extra all around the edge; buy extra skeins of medium olive green for the border.

See the Cabbage Cushion on page 12 for the Other Materials needed, and "Finishing techniques" for instructions on how to make up a cushion cover.

APPLETON COLOURS USED

- ■ 976   deep brown (1 skein)
- ● 335   deep khaki (1 skein)
- ◨ 242   khaki green (1 skein)
- T 332   medium brown olive (1 skein)
- O 331   pale brown olive (1 skein)
- ■ 544   medium olive green (5 skeins)
- ＼ 253   light olive green (3 skeins)
- — 541   light grey green (1 skein)
- □ 421   pale grass green (1 skein)
- + 331A   pale grey green (1 skein)
- N 963   medium grey (1 skein)
- · 961   pale grey (1 skein)
- □ 991   off-white (5 skeins)
- 4 203   dusty rose (1 skein)
- Z 973   medium brown (1 skein)
- ∩ 982   light brown (1 skein)
- ■ 971   medium beige (2 skeins)
- S 988   pale beige (3 skeins)
- ▼ 902   golden brown (1 skein)
- ■ 842   medium gold (1 skein)
- □ 996   light gold (1 skein)
- X 552   lemon (1 skein)

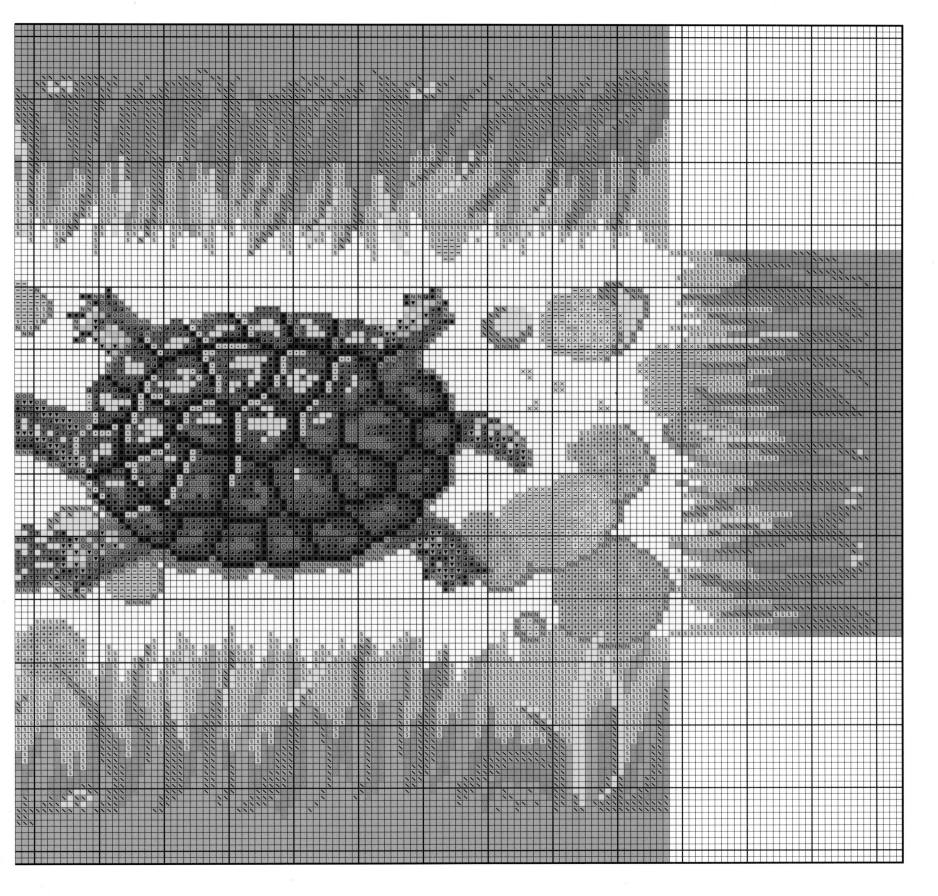

BEGONIA CUSHION

Twenty-five years ago I painted a mural at Arthington Hall, in Yorkshire, which included this begonia among many other tropical flowers. I am especially fond of this plant, as it brings back memories of painting in the limewashed greenhouses of the walled garden. I thought that it would make an excellent subject for a large cushion.

Canvas: 10-gauge double-thread canvas
60 × 60 cm (24 × 24 in)
Tapestry needle size: 18
Approximate finished size: 44.5 × 45 cm
(17½ × 17¾ in)
Embroidery threads:
DMC Laine Colbert tapestry wool

Other materials: Ruler or tape measure
Masking tape • Scissors • Thimble • Pencil
Backing fabric • Matching thread
Cushion pad • Zipper (optional) • Cord
furnishing trim (optional)

STITCHING THE DESIGN

The design is 175 stitches wide by 177 stitches high. Work the design in tent stitch, following the chart and using one strand of wool. Work the foreground first, then fill in the background. Block the completed canvas and finish the cushion as explained in "Finishing techniques".

DMC COLOURS USED

◄ 7108 dark coral (1 skein)

▨ 7125 medium coral (2 skeins)

◥ 7214 light coral (3 skeins)

▢ 7853 pale coral (2 skeins)

▢ 7450 off-white (2 skeins)

< 7520 beige (2 skeins)

U 7509 light brown (4 skeins)

▨ 7524 medium brown (4 skeins)

▨ 7355 dark brown green (2 skeins)

T 7377 dark khaki green (1 skein)

□ 7364 medium khaki green (1 skein)

▲ 7988 medium grass green (4 skeins)

▨ 7548 light grass green (7 skeins)

▨ 7361 light grey green (7 skeins)

↑ 7422 pale green (3 skeins)

N 7470 pale khaki (1 skein)

· 7715 pale grey blue (8 skeins)

▨ 7301 light blue (17 skeins)

✓ 7799 medium blue (5 skeins)

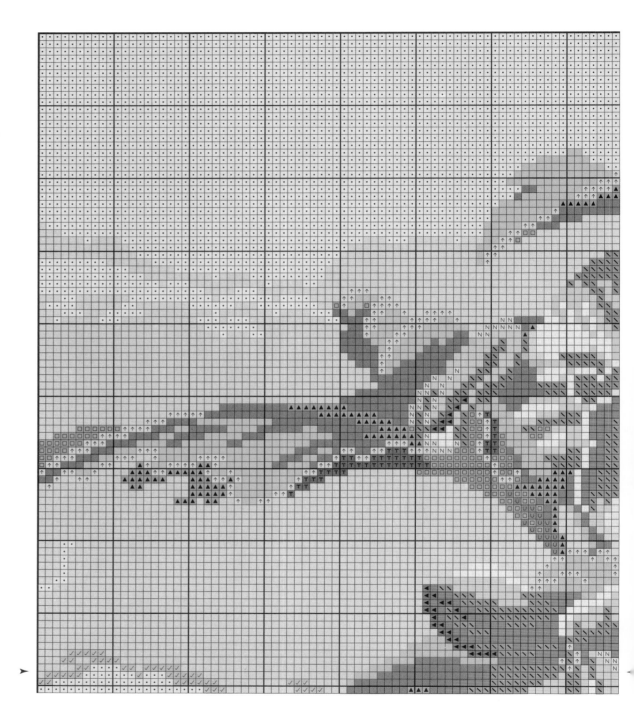

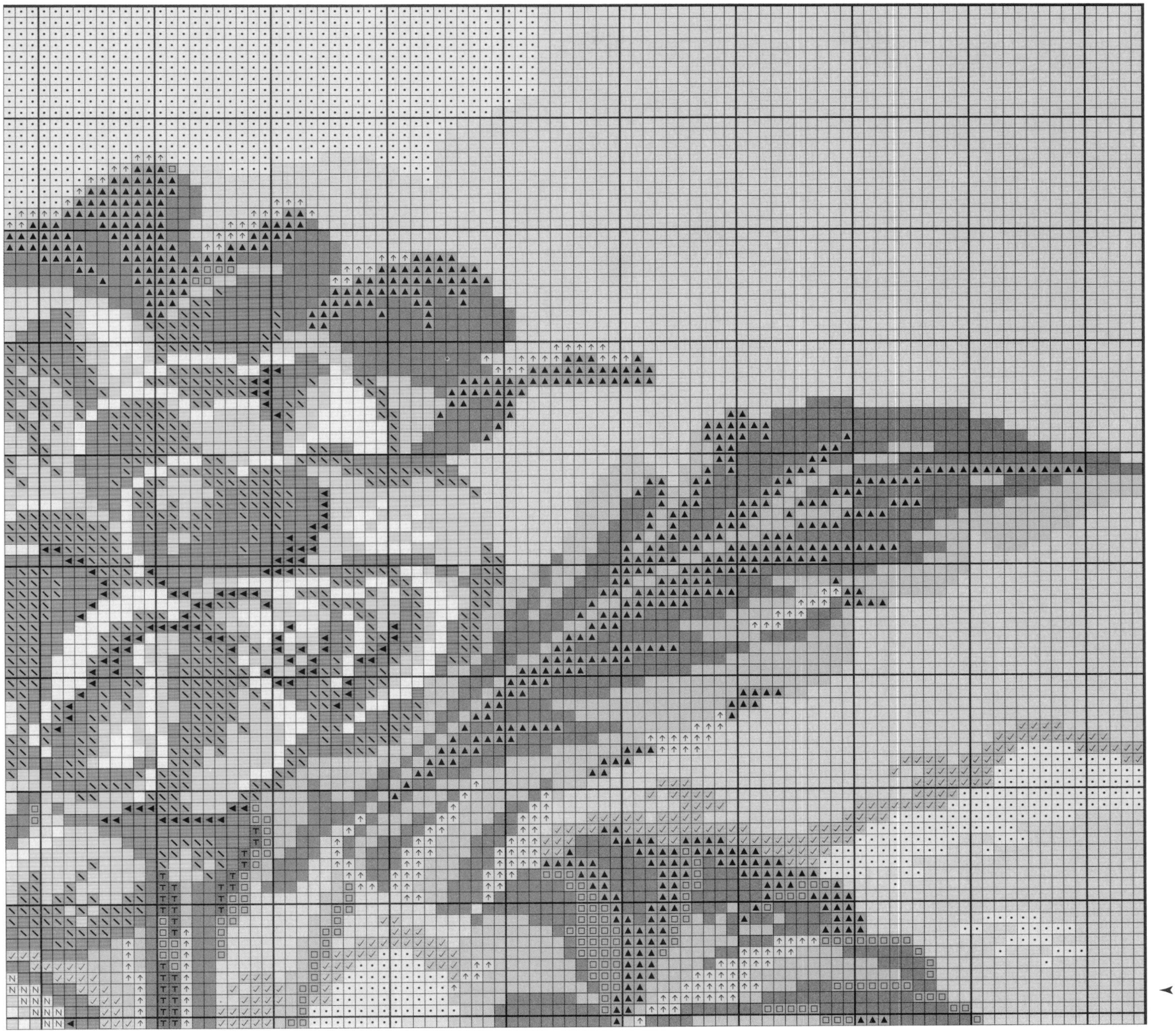

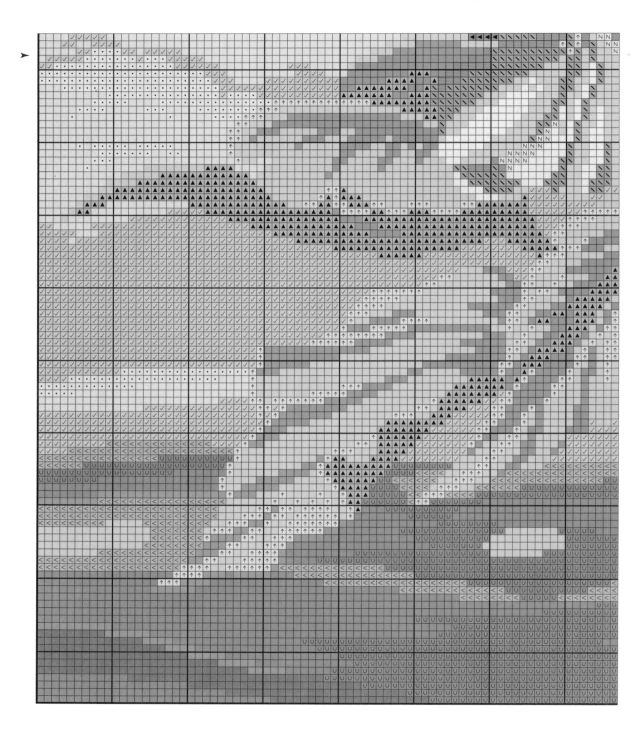

BAT AND MOON EVENING BAGS

These evening bags are large enough to
carry those essential bits and pieces,
but small enough to be elegant.
I have chosen to decorate one
with a classic crescent moon and
stars, and the other with a bat.
The bat is a true creature of the night.
Fortunately, I am very fond of them as there are bats living in my house
in the country and they are often to be seen swooping
across the night sky on summer evenings.
The moon design is more traditional.
The face, of course, represents the Man in the
Moon. If you wish, you could exchange
either of these patterns for your sign
of the zodiac, but keep the same silvery-blue
colours that suit night-time so well.

BAT

Canvas: 10-gauge double-thread canvas
33.5 × 33.5 cm (13¼ × 13¼ in)
Tapestry needle sizes: 22 and 18
Approximate finished size:
18.5 × 18.5 cm (7¼ × 7¼ in)
Embroidery threads:
DMC Médicis crewel wool

Other materials: Ruler or tape measure
Masking tape • Scissors • Thimble
Pencil • Lining and backing fabric
Matching thread • Cord for bag strap

MOON

Canvas: 10-gauge double-thread canvas
33.5 × 33.5 cm (13¼ × 13¼ in)
Tapestry needle sizes: 22 and 18
Approximate finished size:
18.5 × 18.5 cm (7¼ × 7¼ in)
Embroidery threads:
DMC Médicis crewel wool

Other materials: Ruler or tape measure
Masking tape • Scissors • Thimble
Pencil • Lining and backing fabric
Matching thread • Cord for bag strap

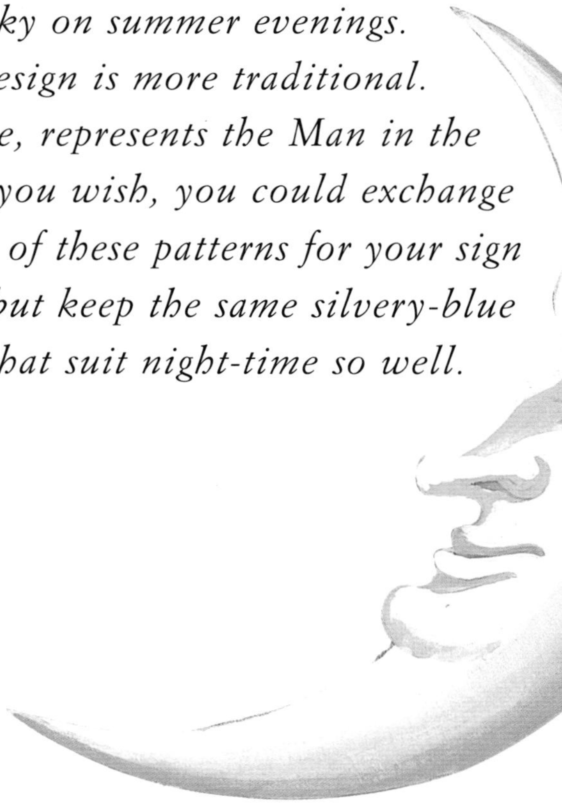

BAT

STITCHING THE DESIGN

The design is worked in both *gros point* and *petit point*. First, stitch the bat and other details in *petit point*, following the chart and using two strands of crewel wool. To work *petit point*, split the double-thread canvas and work each tent stitch over a single canvas thread (20 stitches per inch/2.5 cm).

When the *petit point* is complete, fill in the background in *gros point*, using four strands of crewel wool and working each tent stitch over a double-thread intersection (10 stitches per inch/2.5 cm). (Note that for the *gros point*, four chart squares equal a single stitch.) When the background *gros point* is complete, fill in the remaining *petit point* around the *petit point* details using the background colours.

Block the completed canvas and make the bag as explained in "Finishing techniques".

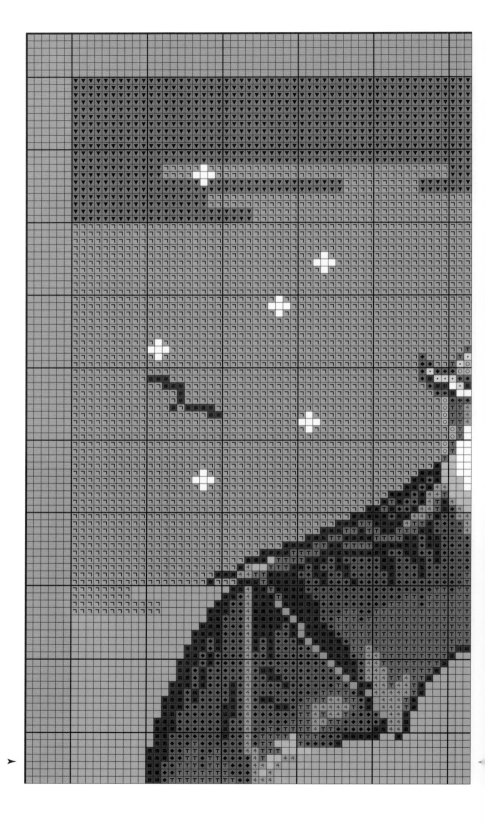

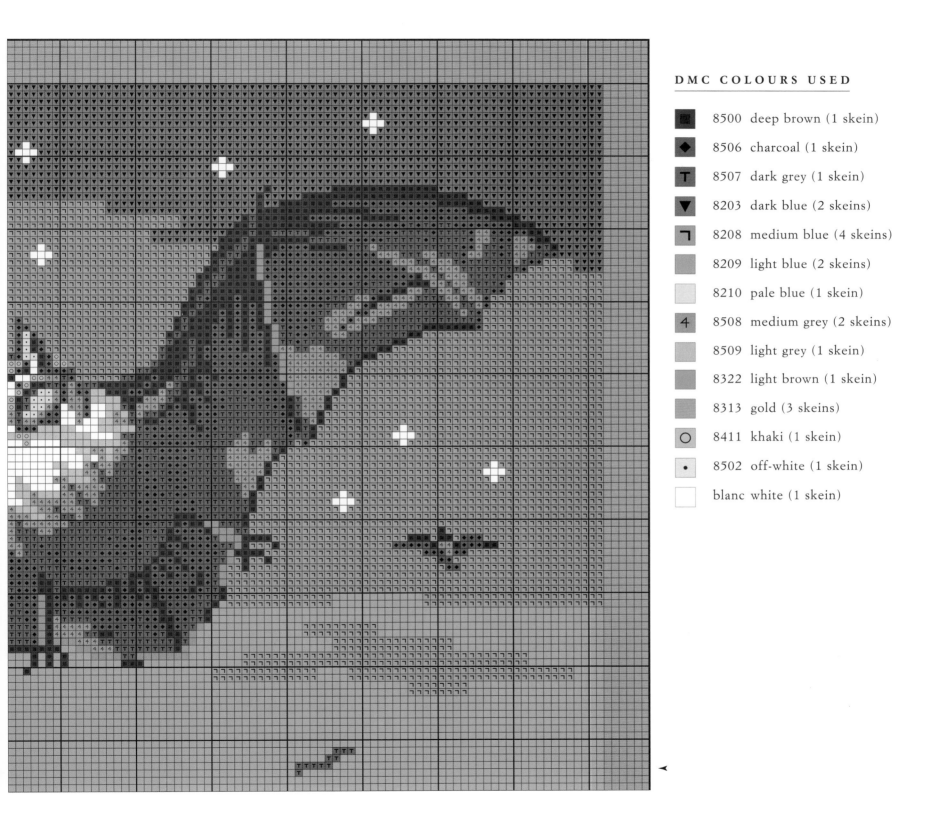

DMC COLOURS USED

▦	8500	deep brown (1 skein)
◆	8506	charcoal (1 skein)
T	8507	dark grey (1 skein)
▼	8203	dark blue (2 skeins)
⌐	8208	medium blue (4 skeins)
	8209	light blue (2 skeins)
	8210	pale blue (1 skein)
4	8508	medium grey (2 skeins)
	8509	light grey (1 skein)
	8322	light brown (1 skein)
	8313	gold (3 skeins)
○	8411	khaki (1 skein)
•	8502	off-white (1 skein)
	blanc	white (1 skein)

BAT *continued*

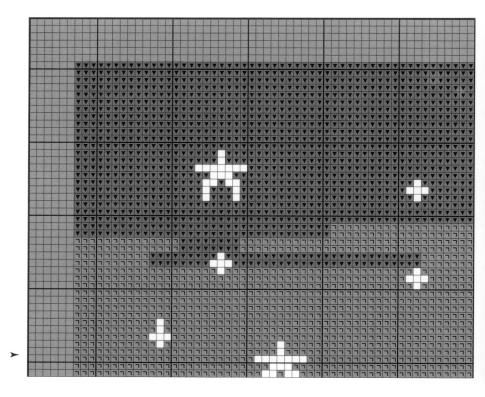

MOON

STITCHING THE DESIGN

The design is worked in both *gros point* and *petit point*. First, stitch the moon and stars in *petit point*, following the chart and using two strands of crewel wool. To work *petit point*, split the double-thread canvas and work each tent stitch over a single canvas thread (20 stitches per inch/2.5 cm).

When the *petit point* is complete, fill in the background in *gros point*, using four strands of crewel wool and working each tent stitch over a double-thread intersection (10 stitches per inch/2.5 cm). (Note that for the *gros point*, four chart squares equal a single stitch.) When the background *gros point* is complete, fill in the remaining *petit point* around the moon and stars using the background colours.

Block the completed canvas and make the bag as explained in "Finishing techniques".

Turn to page 70 for the yarn key.

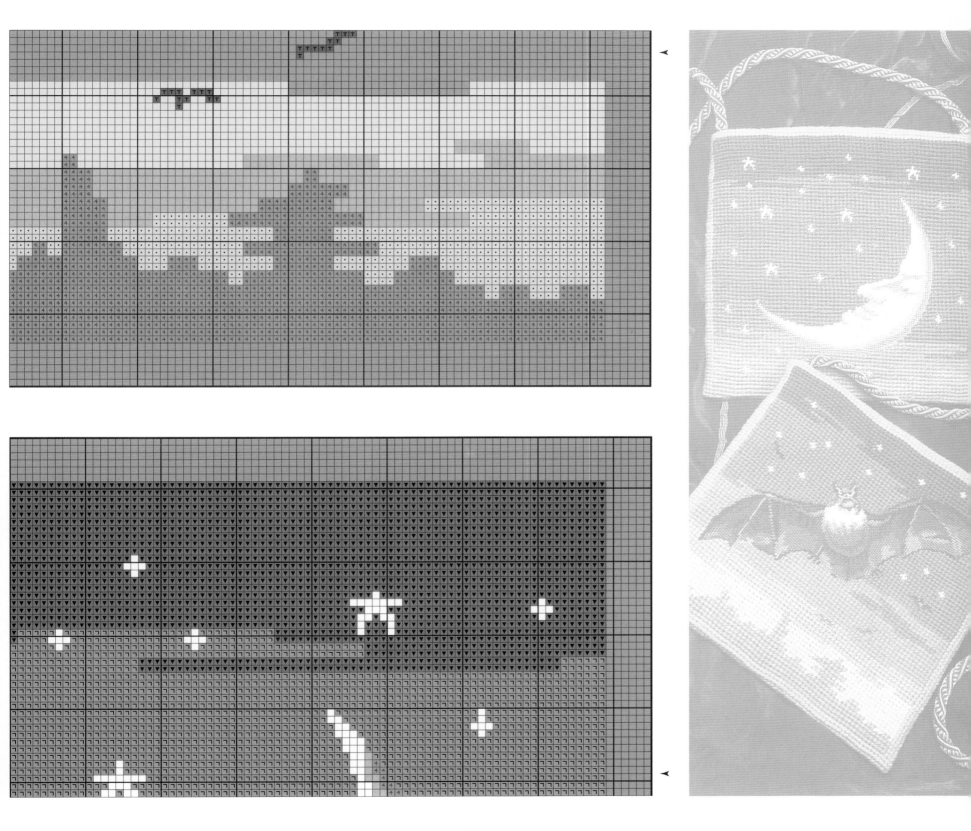

DMC COLOURS USED

- ▼ 8203 dark blue (3 skeins)
- T 8507 dark grey (1 skein)
- ⌐ 8208 medium blue (7 skeins)
- ▦ 8209 light blue (2 skeins)
- ▢ 8210 pale blue (2 skeins)
- 4 8508 medium grey (1 skein)
- ▦ 8509 light grey (1 skein)
- ▢ blanc white (2 skeins)
- ▦ 8313 gold (3 skeins)

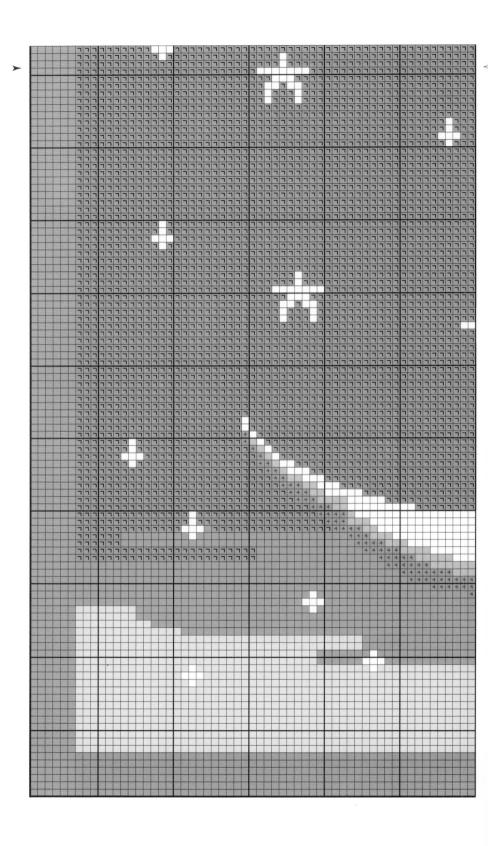

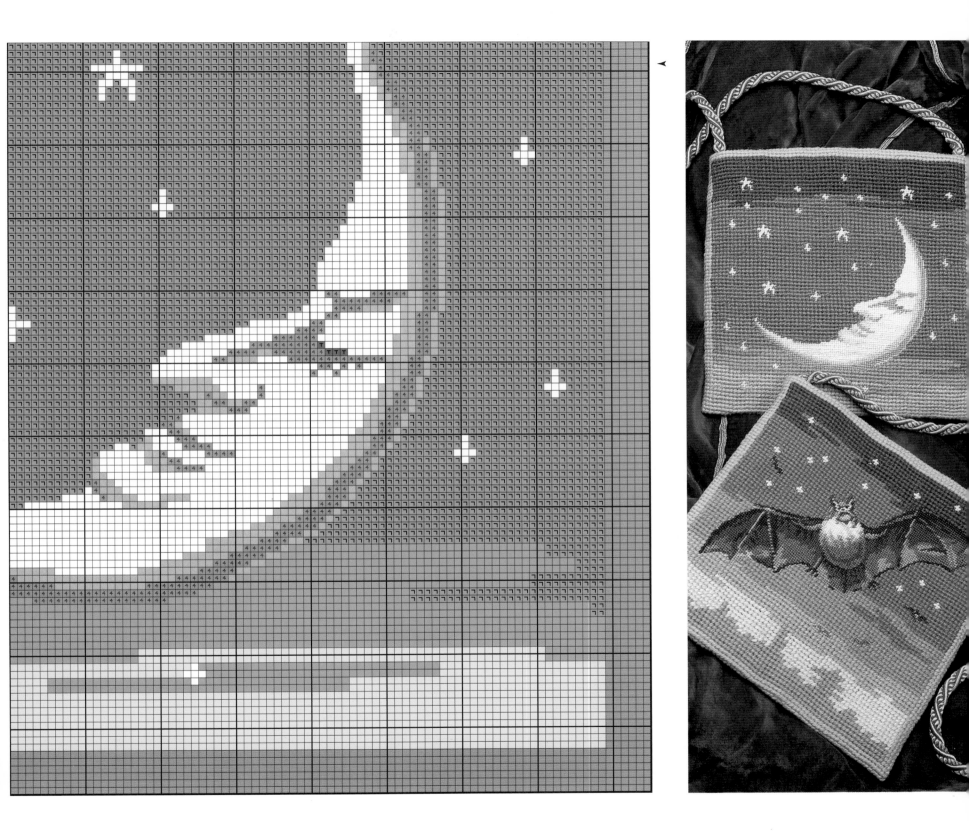

SNAKE SMOKING CAP

The design for this smoking cap shows a tobacco leaf on the top, flat part of the cap and a snake biting its tail around the side. In 1967-68 I was artist-in-residence at Woodberry Forest School in Virginia, and made many drawings of the tobacco plant during my stay. The snake works well as a decorative element as it wraps around the cap as a band. Popular in the late nineteenth century, caps like this one were worn when smoking and relaxing at home. If you don't smoke yourself, you can always use the snake pattern as a belt.

Canvas: 10-gauge double-thread canvas – for a cap, one piece 33 × 33 cm (13 × 13 in) for the circular top and one piece 71 × 20 cm (28 × 8 in) for the rim; for a belt, one piece 122 × 20 cm (48 × 8 in)
Tapestry needle sizes: 22 and 18
Approximate finished size:
top measures 19 cm (7½ in) in diameter, and rim measures 58 cm (23 in), but is adjustable
Embroidery threads: Appleton crewel wool

Other materials: Ruler or tape measure
Masking tape • Scissors • Thimble • Pencil
Lining fabric • Matching thread
Cord furnishing trim with a tassel, for hat only • Buckle, for belt only

STITCHING THE DESIGN

The design for the top of the cap is 74 stitches across the diameter. Work this design in tent stitch, following the chart and using three strands of crewel wool. Work the leaf first, then fill in the background around it.

The design for the side of the cap is worked in both *gros point* and *petit point*. First, stitch the snake in *petit point*, following the chart and using one strand of crewel wool. To work *petit point*, split the double-thread canvas and work each tent stitch over a single canvas thread (20 stitches per inch/2.5 cm).

When the *petit point* is complete, fill in the background and the border in *gros point*, using three strands of crewel wool and working each tent stitch over a double-thread

intersection (10 stitches per inch/2.5 cm). (Note that for the *gros point*, four chart squares equal a single stitch.) Lastly, fill in the remaining *petit point* around the edges of the snake in the background colour.

For a belt, decide on the length needed, and purchase extra yarn. Work the design as for the side of the cap but adjust it so that the snake's head falls where you would like it to. Extend the design to fit the length of your belt.

Block the completed canvases and finish the cap (or belt) as explained in "Finishing techniques". Note that the side of the cap can be reduced in length to fit a smaller adult head circumference, and then the top eased to fit when stitching the two pieces together.

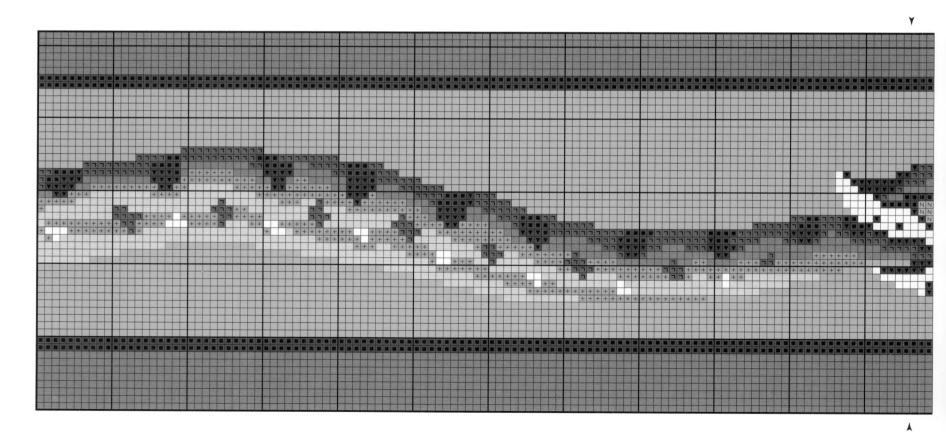

APPLETON COLOURS USED FOR SIDE

- 149 burgundy (4 skeins)
- N 475 gold (1 skein)
- 544 medium green (5 skeins)
- ■ 993 black (2 skeins)
- ▼ 976 charcoal (1 skein)
- ⌐ 965 dark grey (1 skein)
- 964 medium grey (1 skein)
- + 963 light grey (1 skein)
- 989 pastel beige grey (2 skeins)
- □ 991B bright white (1 skein)

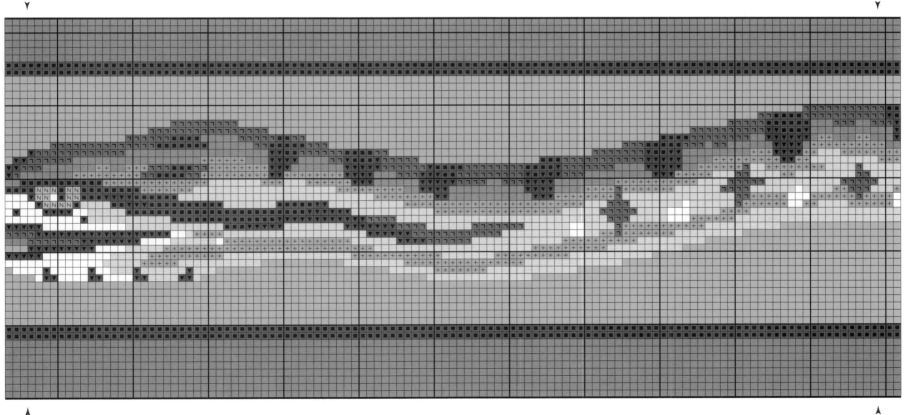

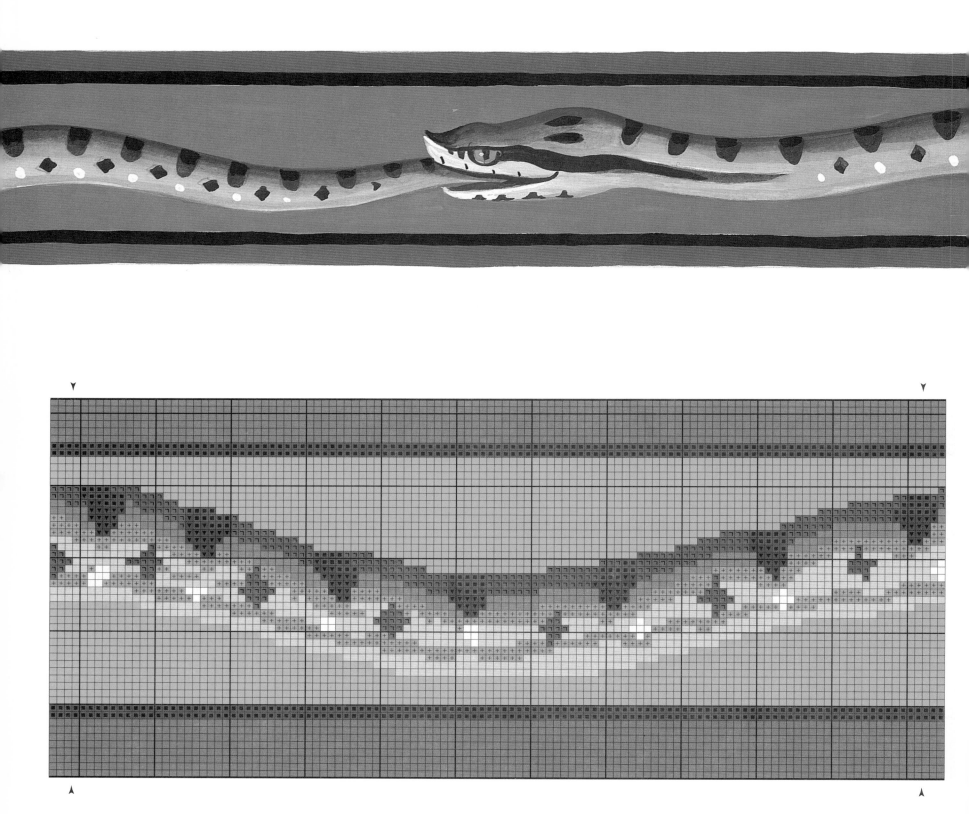

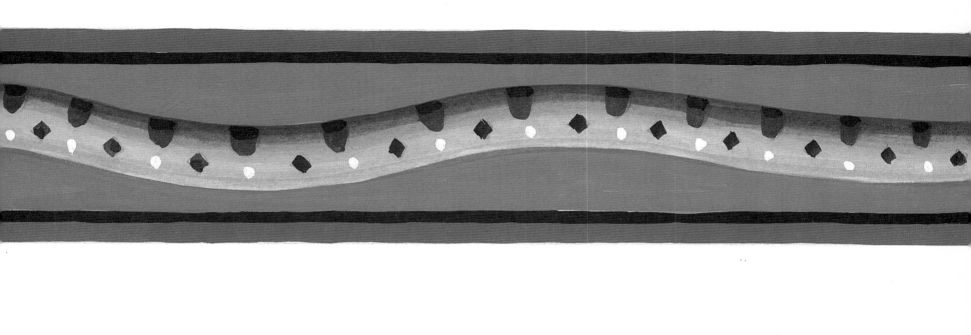

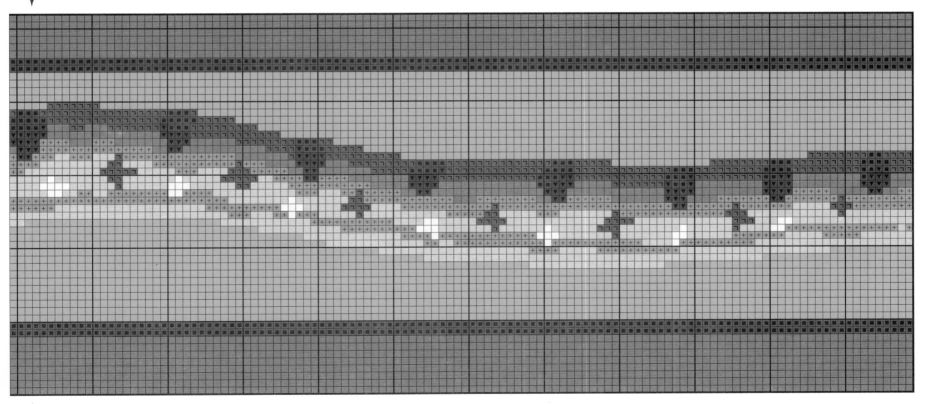

**APPLETON COLOURS
USED FOR TOP**

149   burgundy (5 skeins)

345   dark green (1 skein)

544   medium green (2 skeins)

253   light green (3 skeins)

690   oatmeal (1 skein)

PUG CUSHION

This design is a portrait of a pug named Lindy, who belongs to a friend of mine. There is no reason why you shouldn't create a needlepoint portrait of your own pet by enlarging a photograph and tracing the shape onto the canvas.

Canvas: 10-gauge double-thread canvas
58 × 58 cm (23 × 23 in)
Tapestry needle sizes: 22 and 18
Approximate finished size:
43 × 42 cm (17 × 16¾ in)
Embroidery threads:
Appleton crewel wool

Other materials: Ruler or tape measure
Masking tape • Scissors • Thimble
Pencil • Backing fabric
Matching thread • Cushion pad
Zipper (optional) • Cord furnishing trim
(or filler cord for covering)

STITCHING THE DESIGN

The design is worked in both *gros point* and *petit point*. First, stitch only the dog and the bird in *petit point*, following the chart and using one strand of crewel wool. To work *petit point*, split the double-thread canvas and work each tent stitch over a single canvas thread (20 stitches per inch/2.5 cm).

When the *petit point* is complete, fill in the bowl, the background landscape and sky in *gros point*, using three strands of crewel wool and working each tent stitch over a double-thread intersection (10 stitches per inch/2.5 cm). (Note that for the *gros point*, four chart squares equal a single stitch.) Then work the frame in *gros point*. Next, fill in the remaining *petit point* around the edges of the dog and bird in the background colours.

Work the pastel beige green background (989) outside the circular frame in *gros point*, working it to the extent of the chart and adding 11 stitches extra along the two sides of the embroidery and 15 stitches extra along the top and bottom. Working the outer border stripes in *gros point*, add a line one stitch wide all around the embroidery using light blue green (641), and finally 5 stitches in mid grey green (292) for the outer border.

Block the completed canvas and finish the cushion as explained in "Finishing techniques".

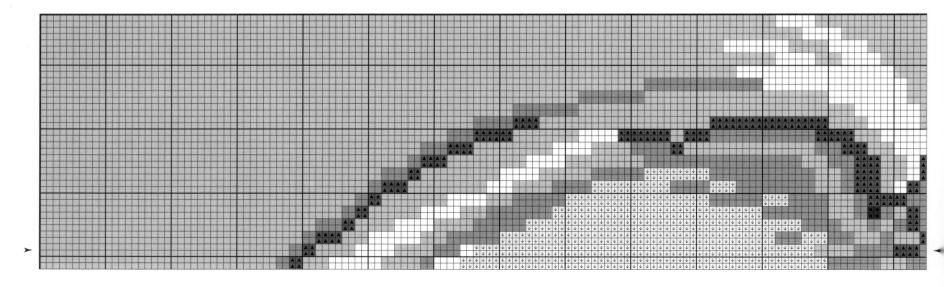

APPLETON COLOURS USED

★	503 dark scarlet (1 skein)	▼	955 golden brown (1 skein)	/	982 light brown (1 skein)
	624 medium coral (1 skein)	□	696 dark gold (1 skein)		989 pastel beige green (24 skeins)
O	142 light dusty rose (1 skein)	F	693 light gold (1 skein)		567 dark blue (1 skein)
	708 pale coral (1 skein)		996 yellow (1 skein)	Z	744 mid blue (1 skein)
<	181 pastel pink beige (1 skein)		984 mid beige (2 skeins)	I	151 light green blue (2 skeins)
×	988 pastel grey beige (1 skein)	C	873 pastel green (1 skein)	↓	875 pastel blue (5 skeins)
	991 off-white (3 skeins)	L	342 mid grey olive (1 skein)	▲	967 charcoal (2 skeins)
	993 black (1 skein)		292 mid grey green (7 skeins)	⌐	973 mid brown (1 skein)
●	584 deep brown (1 skein)	I	352 light grey green (1 skein)	∩	963 mid grey (1 skein)
◆	186 dark brown (1 skein)	▽	641 light blue green (3 skeins)		962 light grey (3 skeins)

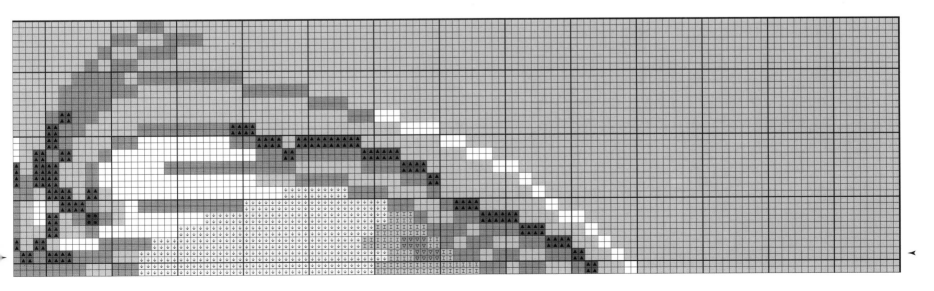

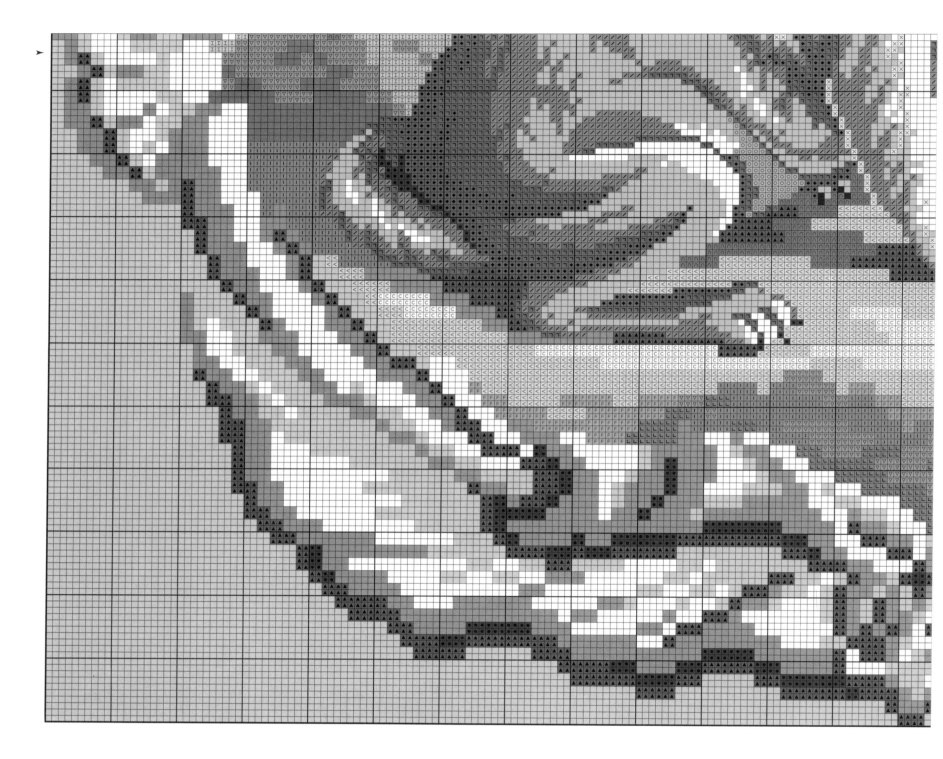

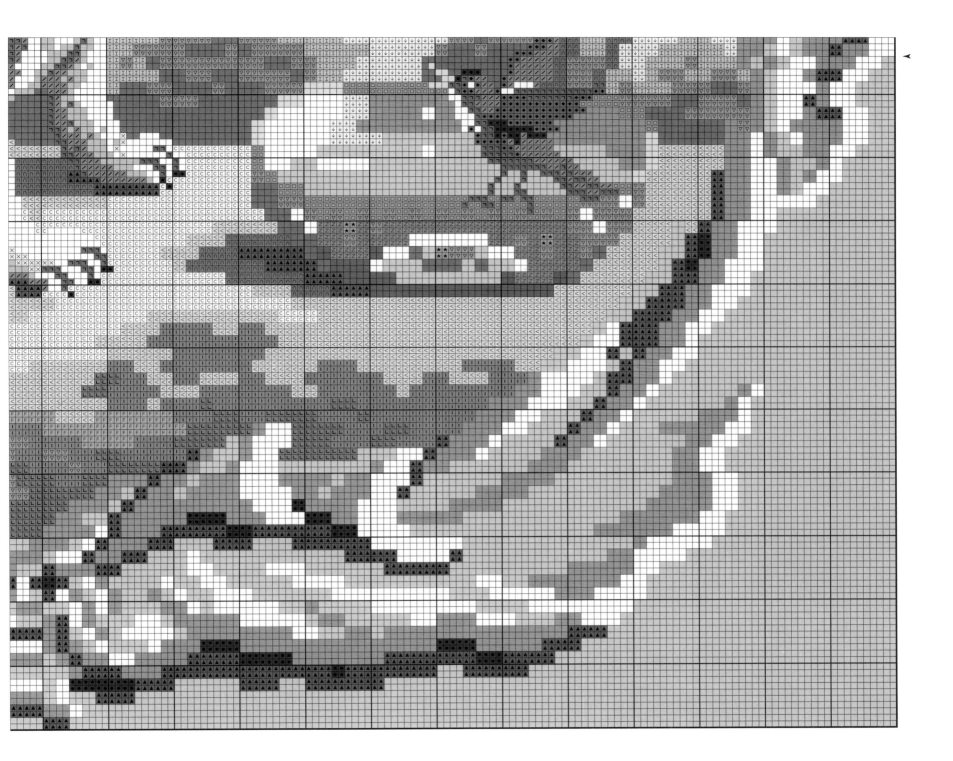

SEASHELLS

Shells are a favourite subject of mine because of their intriguing shapes and subtle gradations of colour. The shells I have at home have been collected over the years from beaches and shops in France and England. The more exotic examples are from Pacific beaches. The patterns given here would make a charming set of cushions, but on page 95 you will see that I have sketched my idea for a rug. If you choose to make the rug, you might like to alternate shells with seaweed or other sea creatures. There are plenty of excellent illustrated guides available from which one can choose shells, coral, seaweed, sea anemones, and so forth. An abstract border based on tangled seaweed holds the various elements together.

Canvas: 10-gauge double-thread canvas, 53 × 53 cm (21 × 21 in) for each design
Tapestry needle size: 18
Approximate finished size of each shell: 37 × 37.5 cm (14½ × 14¾ in)
Embroidery threads: Anchor tapestry wool

Other materials: Ruler or tape measure
Masking tape • Scissors • Thimble
Pencil • Backing fabric • Matching thread
Cushion pad • Zipper (optional)
Cord furnishing trim (optional)

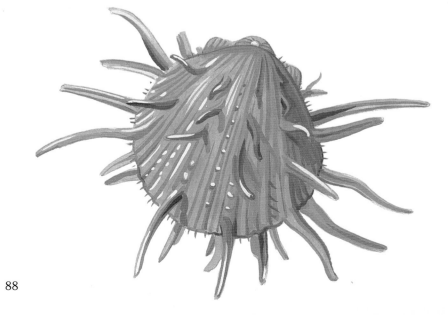

STITCHING THE DESIGN

Each of the designs is 145 stitches wide by 147 stitches high. The designs can be made into a set of cushions or repeated as many times as desired on a large canvas to form a rug. The materials listed on page 88 and the yarn amounts given are for cushions. If you are making a rug, you will need to buy canvas large enough for the rug size and increase the amount of yarn. Advanced needlepointers could add an outer border to their rug following Graham Rust's original sketch shown on page 95. (See also the photograph of the Chinese vases cushion on page 37 for a similar random, background pattern.)

Work each design in tent stitch, following the chart and using one strand of tapestry wool. Work the shell first, then fill in the background and border. Block the completed canvas and make into a cushion or rug as explained in "Finishing techniques".

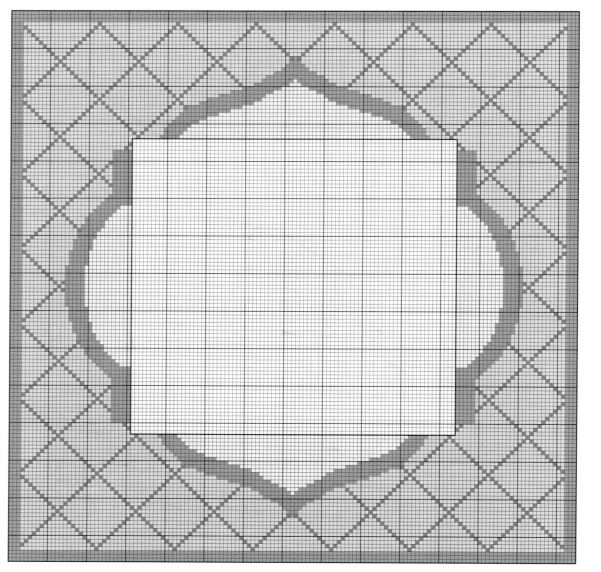

Each of the four Seashell designs fits into the frame shown here. The colours for the frame are included in the yarns keys of the individual shell patterns.

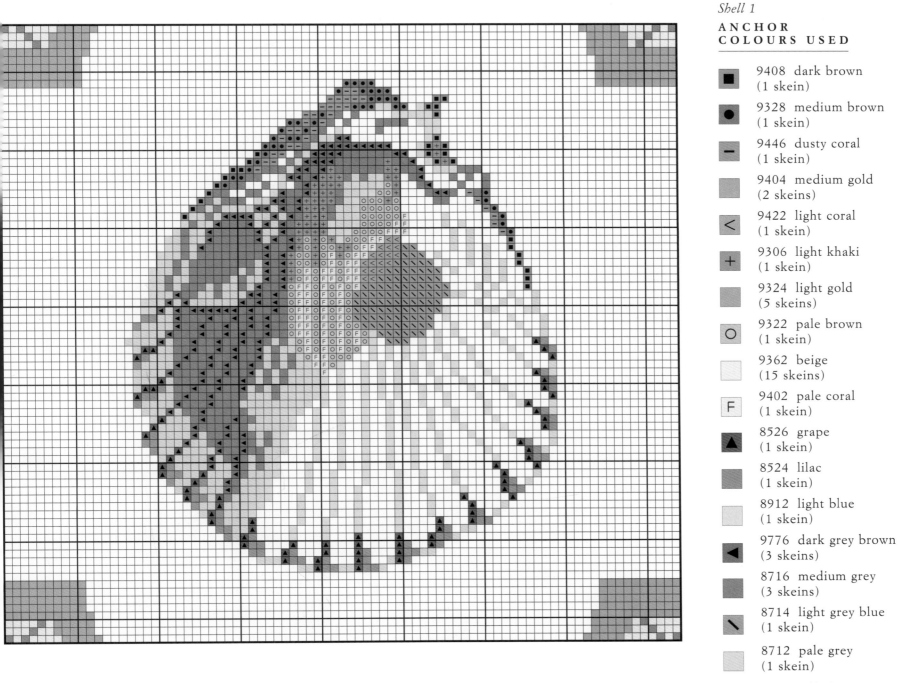

Shell 1

ANCHOR COLOURS USED

■	9408	dark brown (1 skein)
●	9328	medium brown (1 skein)
—	9446	dusty coral (1 skein)
■	9404	medium gold (2 skeins)
<	9422	light coral (1 skein)
+	9306	light khaki (1 skein)
■	9324	light gold (5 skeins)
O	9322	pale brown (1 skein)
	9362	beige (15 skeins)
F	9402	pale coral (1 skein)
▲	8526	grape (1 skein)
	8524	lilac (1 skein)
	8912	light blue (1 skein)
◀	9776	dark grey brown (3 skeins)
	8716	medium grey (3 skeins)
\	8714	light grey blue (1 skein)
	8712	pale grey (1 skein)
	8002	off-white (11 skeins)

Shell 2

**ANCHOR
COLOURS USED**

9404 medium gold
(2 skeins)

9324 light gold
(5 skeins)

9362 beige
(15 skeins)

9308 dark khaki
(1 skein)

8018 mid yellow
(1 skein)

8014 light yellow
(1 skein)

8912 light blue
(1 skein)

8718 dark grey
(1 skein)

8716 medium grey
(2 skeins)

9064 light grey
(1 skein)

8712 pale grey
(1 skein)

8002 off-white
(10 skeins)

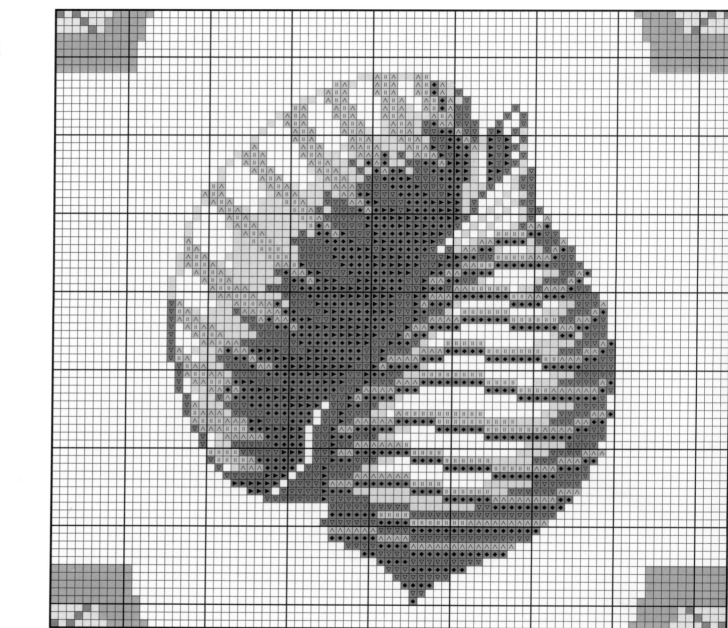

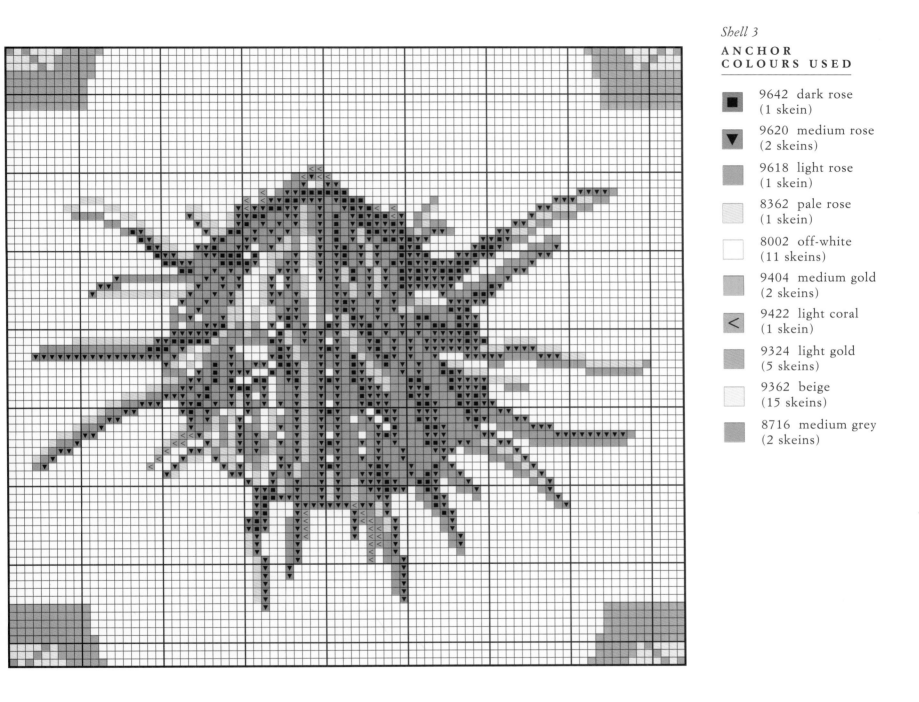

Shell 3

**ANCHOR
COLOURS USED**

9642 dark rose
(1 skein)

9620 medium rose
(2 skeins)

9618 light rose
(1 skein)

8362 pale rose
(1 skein)

8002 off-white
(11 skeins)

9404 medium gold
(2 skeins)

9422 light coral
(1 skein)

9324 light gold
(5 skeins)

9362 beige
(15 skeins)

8716 medium grey
(2 skeins)

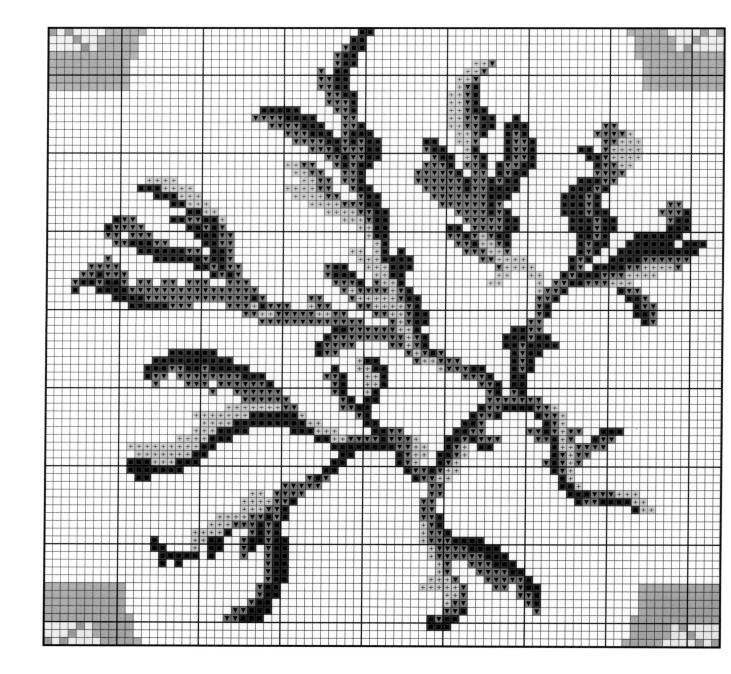

Shell 4

ANCHOR COLOURS USED

9404   medium gold (2 skeins)

9324   light gold (5 skeins)

9362   beige (15 skeins)

8002   off-white (11 skeins)

■   9314   deep khaki (2 skeins)

▼   9328   mid khaki (2 skeins)

+   9062   pale grey-green (1 skein)

8716   medium grey (2 skeins)

See page 90 for suggestions on how to make a rug by combining the Seashell designs and adding an outer border

SUNFLOWER CHAIR

The bold simplicity of this single sunflower lends itself perfectly to a treatment as a chairback. Once you have mastered the sunflower, don't be afraid to seek inspiration from other flowers. A set of dining room chairs can be transformed into something quite charming by the addition of carefully selected blooms. The textured background links the designs, allowing you to choose flowers with contrasting colours. The design for the sunflower chairback would also make a pleasing cushion. Instructions are given in the text for both these options.

Canvas: 12-gauge single-thread canvas 60 × 60 cm (24 × 24 in) for a cushion, or two pieces the required size for a chairback and seat
Tapestry needle size: 18
Approximate finished size: sunflower area measures 32 × 42 cm (12½ × 16½ in) – expand to fit your chair; a sunflower cushion would measure 47 × 47 cm (18½ × 18½ in); petal area measures 28 × 28 cm (11 × 11 in)
Embroidery threads:
DMC Médicis crewel wool

Other materials: Ruler or tape measure
Masking tape • Scissors • Thimble • Pencil

Simple designs, such as this sunflower, are often the most effective

STITCHING THE DESIGN

The sunflower is 151 stitches wide by 197 stitches high. The chart for the petals is 132 stitches wide by 130 stitches high. If you are making a chair cover, first obtain templates for the back and seat from your upholsterer. Trace the template shapes onto the canvas before stitching. The background around the sunflower and petals can be expanded to fill the correct area. You may need to purchase more yarn in the two background colours; the yarn amounts given for the sunflower are for the finished cushion size, which is 47 x 47 cm (18½ in x 18½ in), and for a seat cover 51 x 51 cm (20 x 20 in).

Work the designs in tent stitch, following the chart and using four strands of crewel wool. Work the sunflower first, then work the textured background to the size for the finished square cushion or to the size of the chairback template outline. To work the background, use two strands of off-white (ecru) with two strands of pastel beige (8512) and stitch blocks of tent stitch 10 stitches by 10 stitches, alternating the slant of the tent stitches from block to block to form a chess-board pattern. For a chair cover, work the petals' canvas in the same way. Block the canvases to the size of the original templates, then have the needlepoint stretched onto the chair by your upholsterer.

See page 12 for the Other Materials needed for a cushion. Block the completed canvas, and see "Finishing techniques" for instructions on how to make up a cushion cover.

DMC COLOURS USED FOR THE CHAIRBACK

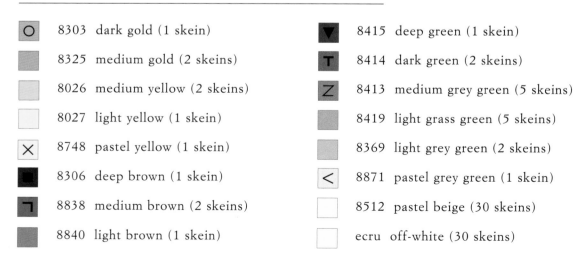

O	8303	dark gold (1 skein)
	8325	medium gold (2 skeins)
	8026	medium yellow (2 skeins)
	8027	light yellow (1 skein)
X	8748	pastel yellow (1 skein)
	8306	deep brown (1 skein)
⌐	8838	medium brown (2 skeins)
	8840	light brown (1 skein)

▼	8415	deep green (1 skein)
T	8414	dark green (2 skeins)
Z	8413	medium grey green (5 skeins)
	8419	light grass green (5 skeins)
	8369	light grey green (2 skeins)
<	8871	pastel grey green (1 skein)
	8512	pastel beige (30 skeins)
	ecru	off-white (30 skeins)

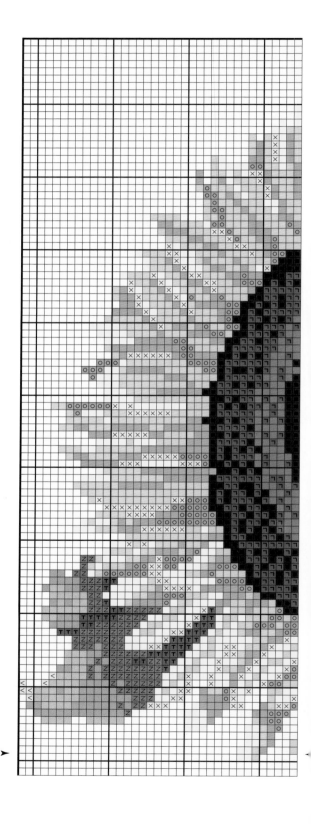

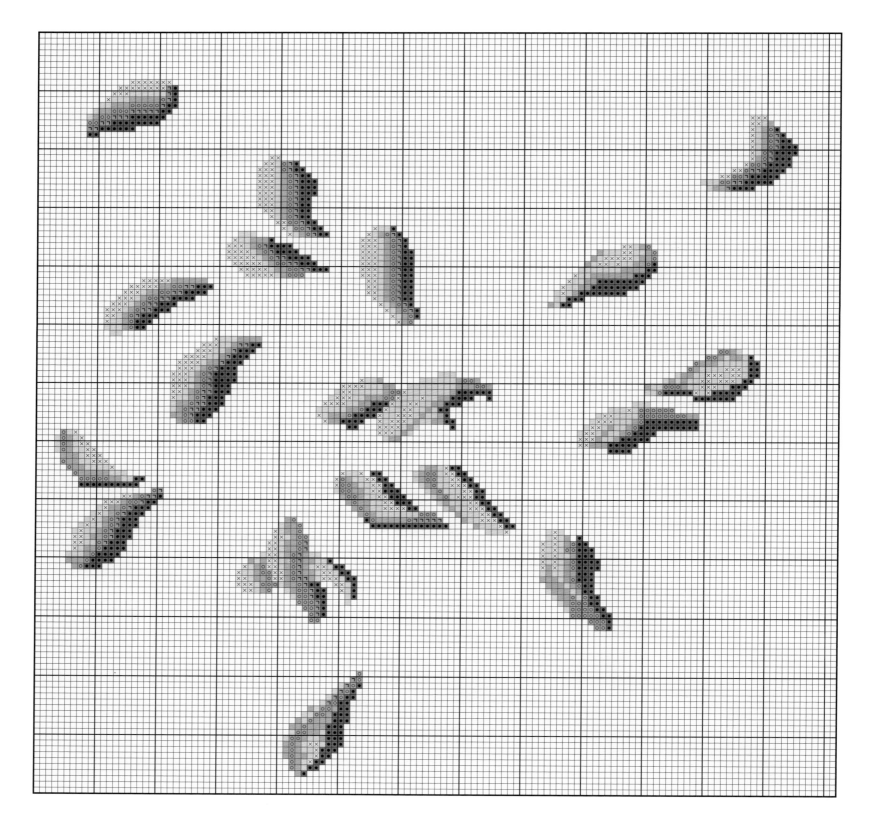

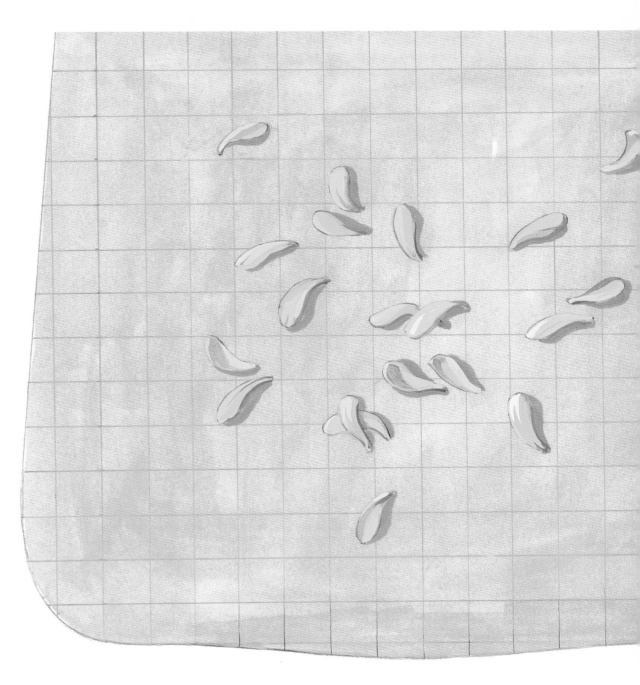

DMC COLOURS USED FOR THE CHAIR SEAT

- ● 8308 tan brown (1 skein)
- ⌐ 8302 cinnamon (1 skein)
- ⊙ 8303 dark gold (1 skein)
- ▧ 8325 medium gold (1 skein)
- ▢ 8026 medium yellow (1 skein)
- ✕ 8748 pastel yellow (1 skein)
- ▢ 8512 pastel beige (44 skeins)
- ▢ ecru off-white (44 skeins)

STRAWBERRY AND BEE PINCUSHION

I chose this combination of a strawberry and a bee because their sight, sound and smell are so evocative of the summer months. The hum of wild bees is a familiar sound in my garden, as they have a hive in the hollow of an old tree.

Canvas: 10-gauge double-thread canvas
30 × 30 cm (12 × 12 in)
Tapestry needle sizes: 22 and 18
Approximate finished size:
14 × 14.5 cm (5½ × 5¾ in)
Embroidery threads: Appleton crewel wool

Other materials: Ruler or tape measure
Masking tape • Scissors • Thimble
Pencil • Backing fabric • Matching thread
Fabric for inner cushion
Pincushion stuffing • Cord furnishing trim
(or filler cord for covering)

A simple border frames the strawberry design, which I have placed on a striped ground reminiscent of summer lawns

STITCHING THE DESIGN

The design is worked in both *gros point* and *petit point*. First, stitch the strawberry, the bee and the shadow in *petit point*, following the chart and using one strand of crewel wool. To work *petit point*, split the double-thread canvas and work each tent stitch over a single canvas thread (20 stitches per inch/2.5 cm).

When the *petit point* is complete, fill in the background in *gros point*, using three strands of crewel wool and working each tent stitch over a double-thread intersection (10 stitches per inch/2.5 cm). (Note that for the background, four chart squares equal a single stitch.) When the background *gros point* is complete, work the border frame and stripes. Lastly, fill in the remaining *petit point* around the edges of the bee and strawberry in the background colour.

Block the completed canvas and finish the pincushion as explained in "Finishing techniques".

APPLETON COLOURS USED

⊟	226	dark rose (1 skein)
◆	225	mid rose (1 skein)
	755	light rose (1 skein)
	142	pale rose (1 skein)
	991	off-white (2 skeins)
T	863	coral (1 skein)
	473	gold (1 skein)
↑	996	yellow (1 skein)
	402	mid green (3 skeins)
	641	light blue green (2 skeins)
Z	543	light green (1 skein)
	993	black (1 skein)
	965	charcoal (1 skein)
⟍	963	light grey (1 skein)
	886	pale blue grey (1 skein)

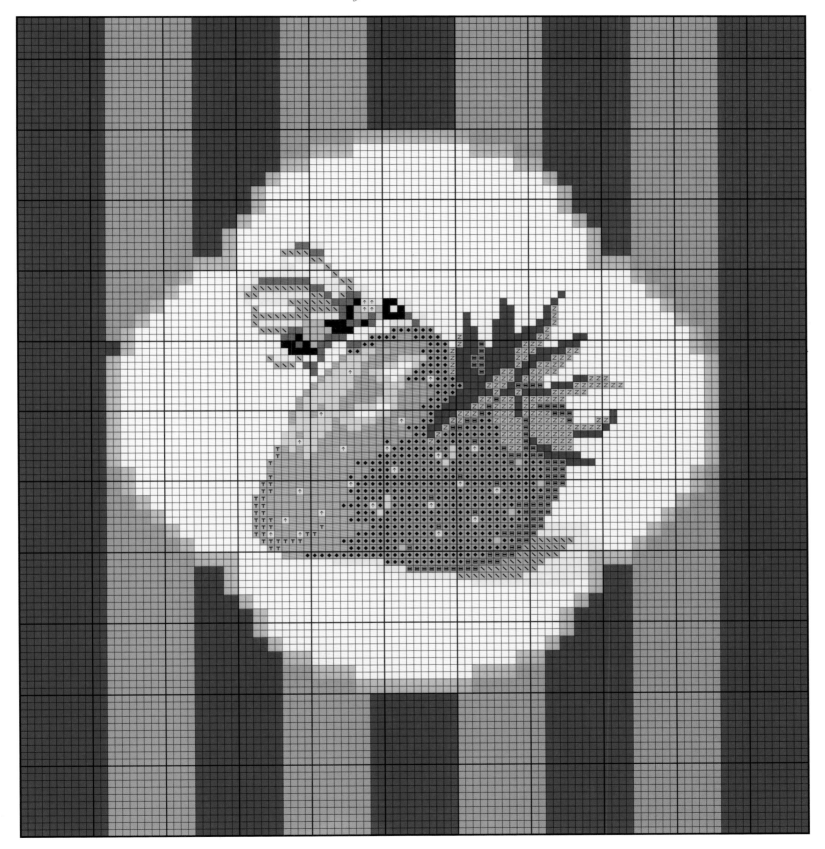

STONE FACE CUSHION

The mask that features in this design is a stone carving that I found in the South of France some thirty years ago. Over the years, many colourful lichens have grown on the brick wall on which the carving hangs. This mask was the inspiration for my very first needlepoint design, which was interpreted directly onto the canvas by a friend, David Cossart.

Canvas: 12-gauge single-thread canvas
60 × 60 cm (24 × 24 in)
Tapestry needle size: 18
Approximate finished size:
46 × 46.5 cm (18 × 18¼ in)
Embroidery threads: Anchor tapestry wool

Other materials: Ruler or tape measure
Masking tape • Scissors • Thimble
Pencil • Backing fabric • Matching thread
Cushion pad • Zipper (optional)
Cord furnishing trim (optional)

The wonderful earth colours of this sketch are translated into a very strong needlepoint design

STITCHING THE DESIGN

The design is 215 stitches wide by 220 stitches high. Work the design in tent stitch, following the chart and using one strand of tapestry wool. Work the face first, then fill in the background. Block the completed canvas and finish the cushion as explained in "Finishing techniques".

Turn to page 112 for the yarn key.

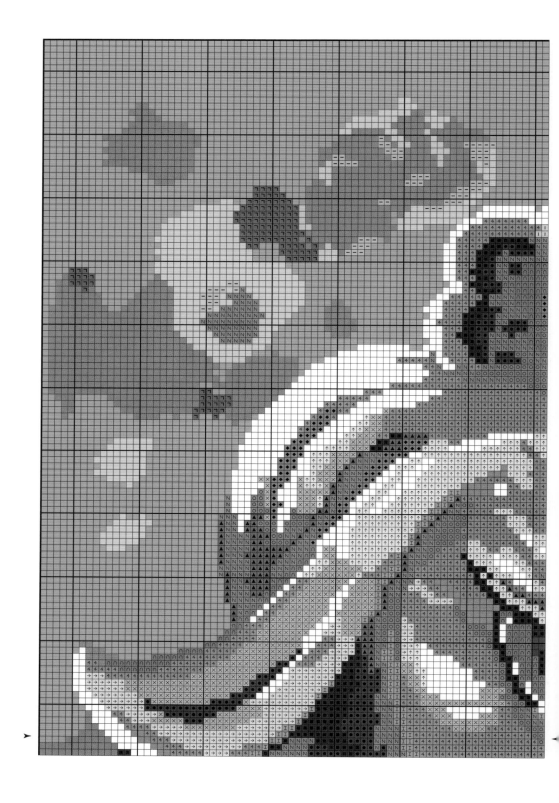

ANCHOR COLOURS USED

■	9666	deep grey brown (4 skeins)
●	9684	deep chocolate brown (2 skeins)
▼	9646	medium brick brown (1 skein)
▲	9682	dark chocolate brown (1 skein)
◆	9450	medium nutmeg (1 skein)
˥	9292	dark khaki brown (2 skeins)
T	9396	deep cinnamon (1 skein)
▨	9798	deep grey (5 skeins)
Z	9392	dark cinnamon (1 skein)
▽	9764	dark grey (4 skeins)
N	9662	mid chocolate brown (3 skeins)
▨	9330	medium khaki (4 skeins)
H	9388	light cinnamon (2 skeins)
I	9390	mid cinnamon (1 skein)
O	9658	light brown (3 skeins)
∩	9794	medium grey (2 skeins)
4	9656	pastel chocolate brown (6 skeins)
▨	9620	dark dusty rose (16 skeins)
▨	9796	light grey (2 skeins)
−	9446	light nutmeg (1 skein)
▨	9326	pale khaki (2 skeins)
I	9672	pastel pink brown (1 skein)
X	9654	pastel coral brown (2 skeins)
→	9634	beige (1 skein)
□	9362	oatmeal (5 skeins)
↑	9052	pastel grey green (3 skeins)

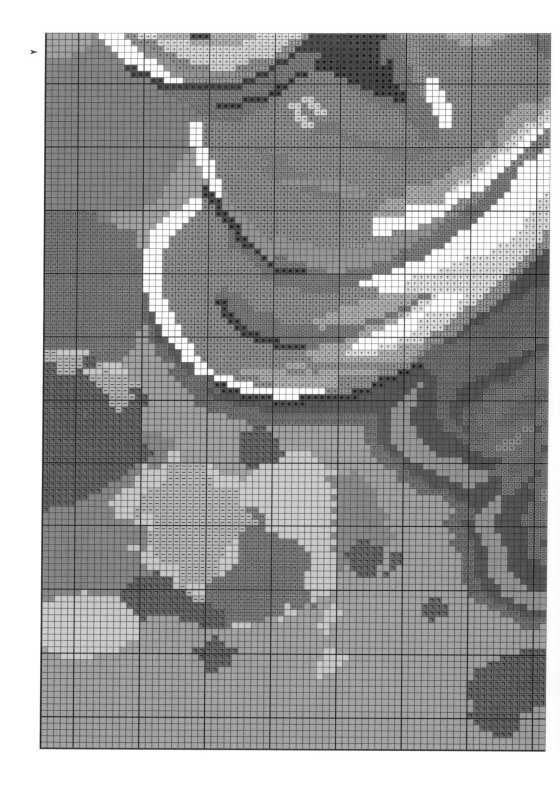

Working and Finishing
needlepoint

WORKING AND FINISHING NEEDLEPOINT

The following techniques and tips are included here as a refresher for experienced needlepointers; they also cover all a beginner needs to know to get started, stitch and finish the projects in this book. You will see that some needlepoint designs have been broken into sections. Where this happens, an arrow indicating repeats is placed at the bottom and top of the charts. Stitch the top section down to the arrow. Stitch the bottom section starting from the arrow; do not stitch the top three lines. Please note that there is no repeat from side to side.

NEEDLEPOINT BASICS

All the needlepoint designs in the preceding pages have been worked in tent stitch, which is a simple, small diagonal stitch worked onto an evenweave needlepoint canvas. The technique can be mastered in minutes. Here are some tips to consider when buying canvas and embroidery threads as well as the basic steps for preparing your canvas and working tent stitch.

Buying needlepoint canvas

Needlepoint canvas is a strong even-weave fabric that has wide gaps between the threads for slipping through the blunt-ended tapestry needle. It comes in a variety of gauges or mesh sizes. The finer gauges have from 16 to 40 holes per inch (2.5 cm); tent stitches worked this tiny are called *petit point*. The coarser gauges range from 10 to 3 holes per inch (2.5 cm) and are used for

working the larger tent stitches, which are called *gros point*.

There are three basic types of needlepoint canvas: single-thread, double-thread and interlocked.

Single-thread canvas is also called mono canvas and has a simple over-and-under construction (see below left). On double-thread canvas, also called Penelope canvas, pairs of fabric threads are grouped together (see below). The

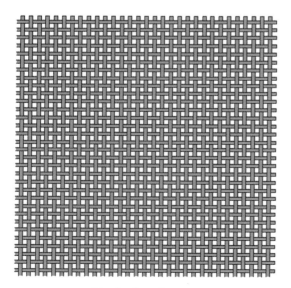

Single-thread canvas

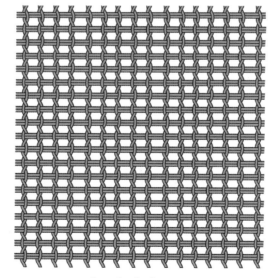

Interlocked canvas

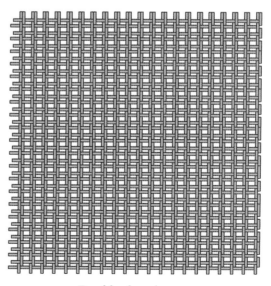

Double-thread canvas

third type is interlocked canvas in which the threads are woven so that they are locked together producing a very stable fabric (see opposite, below centre).

Each type of canvas comes in various gauges, but the very finest gauges are only available in the single-thread version. Interlocked canvas comes in the medium and large range of sizes and is especially popular for the larger stitches used for rugs because of its stability. Double-thread canvas is used when both *petit point* and *gros point* are to be worked in the same design, since the paired threads can be split apart and worked over individually for the finer stitches. Double-thread canvas is also often chosen by embroiderers who wish to work tent stitch using the half-cross method (see half-cross tent stitch page 118).

Needlepoint project instructions usually recommend what type of canvas you should purchase. If there is no reason that a particular type is necessary, such as the use of *petit point* and *gros point* on the same canvas, experienced needlepointer should feel free to choose the canvas they feel most comfortable working with.

The size of canvas required is also given in the needlepoint instructions. It allows for between 5 cm and 7.5 cm (2 to 3 in) of extra canvas all around the design. This extra canvas is useful for stretching and blocking the completed embroidery.

When buying your canvas you will find that it comes in a few neutral shades, the most usual being white and ecru. What colour you choose is up to you, but it is better to use ecru for designs worked in very dark colours, since a glaring white canvas might show through the odd tiny gap between the embroidery threads.

Buying needlepoint threads

All except one of the designs in this book are worked in wool needlepoint threads. The exception is the Frog Pincushion (see pages 26–29), which is worked in stranded cottons. Wool threads are the most popular for needlepoint. They are easier to use than other types of fibres and are available in an enormous range of colours and several weights. They are also very long lasting and durable and require infrequent cleaning since they resist moisture and dust very successfully.

The weights of wool needlepoint threads that are used most often are: crewel, Persian and tapestry. Crewel wool is a strong yarn fine enough to use for the delicate *petit point*. It is also suitable for larger gauge canvases if several strands are used together in the needle; for this reason, it is a good choice for designs that combine *petit point* and *gros point*.

Persian yarn is slightly thicker than crewel wool and usually comes as three strands twisted together. These threads

can be separated and used singly for *petit point*, or separated and recombined for larger stitches and gauges.

Tapestry wool is the yarn that is most frequently used for needlepoint since it is suitable for the larger canvas meshes. Used singly it will cover both 10- and 12-gauge canvases, and two or more strands together will cover 3- to 8-gauge "rug" canvases.

Your needlepoint instructions will always recommend the brand and type of threads to use and quote the shade numbers and quantities required, as well as the number of strands to use for a particular gauge of canvas. It is advisable to try to purchase the recommended brand since these are the colours the designer has used and because the skein amounts might have to be recalculated if a different thread is used. For information on using alternative yarns, see page 130.

Preparing the canvas

Before beginning to work a needlepoint design, it is a good idea to mark the outline of the design on the canvas. When working from a chart, count the number of stitches in each direction across the design. Each square on the chart represents a single tent stitch which is to be worked over a canvas intersection. Count the canvas intersections in each direction, and centring the design on the canvas, mark the outline using a pencil, a water-soluble pen or basting thread. Trace this outline from the canvas onto a piece of paper to use as a template to block the finished embroidery back into shape.

Your embroidery canvas can be mounted on a large rectangular frame for stitching if desired. The canvas is firm enough to be embroidered in the hand, and you will find it very convenient to be able to carry your work around with you to stitch during spare moments. If you do intend to work the canvas in the hand, fold masking tape over the raw edges to prevent them from fraying during stitching.

Choosing a tent stitch technique

A variety of stitches can be worked on needlepoint canvas, but small, diagonal tent stitches are the most versatile. All of the designs in this book are worked in tent stitch.

Tent stitch can be formed in three different ways. Each of the three techniques produces the same slanting stitch on the front of the canvas, and only the reverse side of the work reveals the method used to create the stitches.

The way you work tent stitch is entirely up to you. If you have never worked tent stitch before, try each of the three techniques – continental, basketweave and half-cross – before deciding which one you prefer. You can use one, two or all three techniques on the same canvas, but large solid-

coloured areas such as backgrounds should be worked in the same method throughout to avoid visible ridges forming on the right side of the work.

For all the methods, use threads no longer than 46 cm (18 in) in length. Longer threads are hard to handle and will fray and split before they are used up. Never knot a thread, either at the beginning or the end of the work. Also, use a blunt-ended tapestry needle in a thickness that passes easily through the canvas holes. Needle sizes are given with the needlepoint instructions.

Working continental tent stitch

When tent stitch is worked using the continental method, long diagonal stitches that completely cover the canvas are formed on the wrong side. This technique can be worked on any

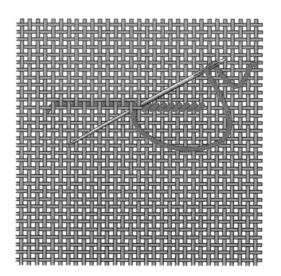

Working the first row of continental tent stitch

type of needlepoint canvas. Thread the tapestry needle with the specified thread and the required number of strands. Then, working the first few stitches over the thread end at the back, work from right to left inserting the needle under two canvas

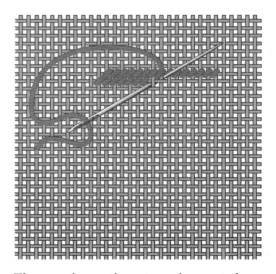

The second row of continental tent stitch

intersections for each stitch as shown. Work the following row in the opposite direction as shown. If desired, you can turn the canvas upside down after each row so that you are always working in same direction. Thread the end of each length of yarn through the slanting stitches on the wrong side.

Working half-cross tent stitch

Half-cross tent stitch is so called because it is worked in the same way as the first arm of two-journey cross stitch. This method can only be worked successfully on double-thread or interlocked canvas, since the straight vertical stitches formed on the wrong side of the canvas can slip through single-thread weaves. It produces a less bulky needlepoint than the other two techniques because the stitches on the reverse form vertical lines between the canvas threads and do not cover the canvas. For this reason it uses less thread than the other two methods.

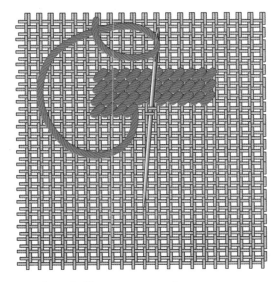

Working half-cross tent stitch

Using the specified thread and the required number of strands, make short vertical stitches to form the diagonal tent stitches as shown above. Work the first few stitches over the loose end of thread at the back of the canvas as for the continental method. Work the rows alternately from left to right and from right to left. When a length of embroidery thread is used up, weave the end through the stitches at the back to secure it.

Working basketweave tent stitch

This tent stitch technique gets its name from the basketweave pattern formed on the wrong side. It is often the technique of preference for working large areas of solid-coloured background since it produces a very stable fabric. Like the continental method, it uses more thread than the half-cross technique.

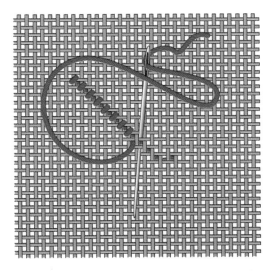

Working basketweave tent stitch downwards

Thread the tapestry needle as for the continental method. Working the first few stitches over the thread end, insert the needle vertically under two canvas threads for each stitch of the first downward diagonal row as shown.

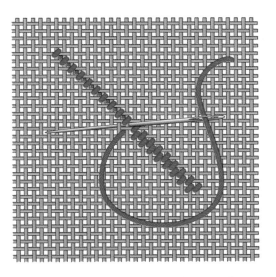

Working basketweave tent stitch upwards

Work the following row upwards, fitting the stitches in between those of the previous row and inserting the needle horizontally under two canvas threads for each stitch as shown. Continue in this way, working the diagonal rows alternately upwards and downwards. Weave the end of each length of yarn through the basketweave stitches on the wrong side.

Blocking finished embroideries

When complete, your embroidery will need to be stretched or blocked into its true shape as it will have become distorted, even if worked in a frame. You will need a piece of plywood or fibre-board at least 10 cm (4 in) larger all around than the piece of embroidery. Tape white blotting paper or a piece of old white sheet over the board. Using a pencil and a ruler, draw the template outline (prepared before the canvas was stitched) onto the paper or sheet.

Lay the embroidery face down on the board and slightly dampen the wrong side, applying the water with a plant spray or a sponge. With the needlepoint still face down, nail it to the board through the unworked canvas border using carpet tacks.

Following the design outline, begin at one corner and work outwards in both directions spacing the tacks no more than 2.5 cm (1 in) apart. Continue all around the embroidery.

Check to make sure that the stretched work is square and taut and then dampen thoroughly. Leave the embroidery to dry naturally for two to three days before removing the tacks. If it still seems out of shape, repeat the blocking process until it is completely flat and square.

Blocking the finished embroidery on a board

FINISHING TECHNIQUES

Once your needlepoint is completed and has been blocked into shape, it is ready to be made up into whatever it is destined to be. With the exception of the upholstering skills required for covering chairs or footstools, the finishing techniques that follow require only basic sewing know-how.

Having a sewing machine is not absolutely necessary, but items such as a cushion cover or an evening bag will be stronger if stitched together by machine. If you do not have a sewing machine or if sewing is not one of your strong points, you might find that your local needlecraft shop provides the service of both blocking and finishing completed needlepoints.

Making a cushion cover

The various materials you will need for making your cushion cover are listed with the project instructions. For the backing fabric, you should choose a strong furnishing fabric that either matches the colour of the needlepoint background or border, or tones in with the embroidery in another way without detracting from the design.

Although a simple cover can be made and stitched closed after the cushion pad has been inserted, including a zipper will make the cover more easily removable. Purchase a zipper that matches the backing fabric and measures about

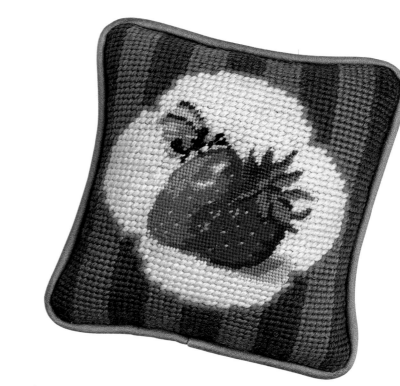

7.5 cm (3 in) shorter than the width of the finished blocked embroidery.

A cushion cover is definitely enhanced by the addition of a cord around the edge covering the seam. Take your completed embroidery with you when choosing the cord so that you can test it against the design. You can also make your own corded edge by covering a piping cord with the backing fabric.

Before backing the cushion cover, trim the unworked canvas around the blocked embroidery to 2 cm (3/4 in). If you intend to pipe the edge of the cushion, make up enough piping to go around the cushion with an extra 10 cm (4 in) to allow for the overlap.

Begin the piping by cutting strips of fabric on the bias that are wide enough

to wrap around the piping cord and leave seam allowances of 2 cm (3/4 in) and that are long enough once joined to cover the length of cord required.

Join the strips together with the right sides facing and stitch with the grain of the fabric.

Basting fabric over piping cord

Fold the bias-cut strip over the cord aligning the raw edges, and baste the strip in place stitching close to the piping cord.

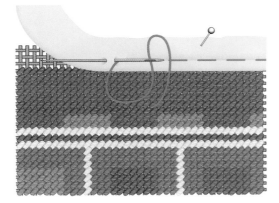

Basting the piping cord to the canvas

Next, pin then baste the piping cord around the right side of the embroidery, starting at the centre of the bottom edge and aligning the basting with the edge of the tent stitches.

Where the ends of the piping meet, trim them so that they overlap by 2.5 cm (1 in). Then roll back the bias covering on one end and cut 2.5 cm (1 in) off the end of the cord so that the cords will just meet. Turn under the end of the extended bias strip, and slip the other end of the piping neatly inside. Stitch the folded edge of the overlapping cover in place so that the ends are joined. (Note that decorative cord with a seam insertion tape can be attached to the cover in the same way as piping, but where the ends meet they should be sloped into the seam.)

Next, prepare the back of the cover. For a back without a zipper, cut a piece of backing fabric to the exact size of the blocked and trimmed canvas.

For a back with a zipper, cut a piece of backing fabric to the same width as the blocked and trimmed canvas but 4 cm (1½ in) longer. Fold the fabric in half widthways and cut apart along the fold, then fold and press 2 cm (¾ in) to the wrong side along both of these cut edges. Unfold the pressed-under seam allowances and pin the pieces together, right sides facing. Hand or machine stitch each end of the seam together, leaving an opening for the zipper.

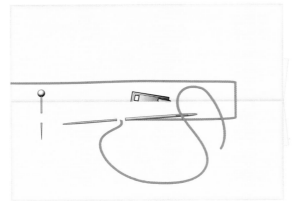

Inserting a zipper in a cushion cover

Re-press the seams open and pin the zipper in place inside the opening. Stitch the zipper in position by hand using backstitch, or machine stitch using a zipper foot.

Pin the back and the front of the cushion cover together with right sides facing. Backstitch the seam, or machine stitch using a zipper foot if piping is being attached. If there is no zip, leave an opening on one side of the cover for inserting the cushion pad.

Trim the seam corners, and turn the cover right side out, easing out the corners. Insert the cushion pad through the zipper opening or the opening in the edge seam. Then close the zipper or slip stitch the opening closed.

If you are attaching a decorative cord without a seam insertion tape, stitch it in place over the cushion edge seam inserting the ends through a small gap in the seam.

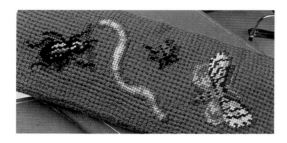

Making a glasses case

For the glasses case on pages 16–19, choose a silky lining fabric that matches the colour of the needlepoint background. Before beginning any stitching, trim the unworked canvas around both pieces of blocked embroidery to 1.5 cm (½ in). Cut two pieces of lining to the same size as the trimmed canvas and set aside.

Carefully fold the unworked canvas to the wrong side of the embroidery on each of the two pieces of needlepoint, making sure that none of the unworked canvas is visible from the right side. Sew the seam allowances to the back of the work using herringbone stitch.

Next, press the seam allowance on the lining pieces to the wrong side. Then pin one of the lining pieces to one of the needlepoint pieces with wrong sides together, and slip stitch in place. Repeat for the second half of the glasses case.

With the lined sides facing, pin the two halves of the case together making sure that the corners are perfectly aligned. Firmly oversew the two halves together as invisibly as possible, leaving the short, straight end open.

Making a pincushion

A pincushion cover is made in the same way as a cushion cover without a zipper opening. But you will also have to make the inner cushion to hold the stuffing. For the inner cushion, choose a tightly woven neutral coloured fabric.

Before making the inner cushion, trim the unworked canvas around the blocked embroidery to 1.5 cm (½ in). Then cut two pieces of fabric for the cushion pad to the same size as the trimmed canvas. With the right sides facing, pin and stitch the pieces together, taking a 1.5 cm (½ in) seam allowance and leaving a gap for stuffing. Trim the corners of the seam allowances and turn right side out. Stuff the cushion firmly and slip stitch the opening closed.

Next, cut a piece of backing fabric to the same size as the trimmed embroidery. Complete as for a cushion cover without a zipper, attaching piping or decorative cord as desired.

Making a tea cosy

For the tea cosy on pages 30–35, purchase matching lining and backing fabrics, but choose a strong furnishing fabric for the backing and a lightweight cotton for the lining. Make sure that the colour either complements or matches the needlepoint background.

First, trim the unworked canvas around the blocked embroidery to 2 cm (¾ in). Then cut two pieces of lining and one piece of backing to the same size as the trimmed canvas. Cut two pieces of padding to the same size as the lining, omitting the seam allowance all around the pieces.

Pin the backing to the embroidery with right sides facing, and hand or machine stitch together along the curved edge leaving the straight lower edge open. Trim the seam allowances, notch along the curve and turn right side out. Stitch the lining pieces together in the same way, but do not turn right side out.

Insert the padding inside the tea cosy, then the lining. Turn the lower edges on the cosy and the lining to the wrong side, align the folded edges and slip stitch together leaving small gaps at the ends of the seam for tucking the cord inside.

Stitch the decorative cord in place along the seam, tucking the ends inside the lining and forming a loop at the top. Secure the loop at the top by stitching through the top of the cosy and catching in the lining.

Making a footstool or chair cover

Upholstering footstools and chairs is best left to the experts (see pages 48–53 for a footstool design and pages 96–103 for a chair cover design). Professional upholsterers will provide you with a template for your proposed needlepoint and will mount the completed embroidery. The template can be used to draw the outline of the tent stitches onto the needlepoint canvas and as the size guide for blocking the embroidery.

Making a doorstop

Before placing the needlepoint over the brick for the doorstop on pages 54–57, wrap the brick in calico like a parcel and stitch the calico in place.

Next, trim the unworked canvas around the blocked embroidery to 2 cm (³/₄ in). Fold the embroidery with right sides together and firmly stitch each corner seam by hand using backstitch. Trim the seams to 1.5 cm (½ in) and finger-press open.

Turn the cover right side out and place over the brick. With a strong thread, lace the canvas edges of the cover from side to side and from top to bottom, tightening the cover as you go.

Cut a piece of furnishing fabric to the same size as the base of the doorstop plus a seam allowance of 1.5 cm (½ in) all around. Turn under and press the seam allowances, then slip stitch to the bottom edges of the embroidered cover.

Making an evening bag

When choosing the backing for the evening bags on pages 64–71, try to match it to one of the background colours on the needlepoint. A velvet or another strong and luxurious fabric would be suitable as a backing. For the lining choose a contrasting but complementary colour in a silk or a similar shiny fabric.

Trim the unworked canvas around the blocked embroidery to 2 cm (¾ in). Then cut one backing piece and two pieces of lining to the same size as the trimmed canvas. Pin the backing and the embroidery together with right sides facing, and hand or machine stitch, leaving the top edge open and leaving a small gap in the middle of the lower edge for tucking in the ends of the cord trim. Trim the seam allowances and the corners. Then turn right side out.

Stitch the lining pieces together in the same way, but do not leave a gap in the lower edge and do not turn right side out. Slip the lining inside the bag. Turn under the top edges of the lining and the bag, aligning the folds. Pin and slip stitch the lining to the bag.

Stitch the cord in place along the seam, forming the bag strap at the top and slipping the ends inside the gap in the seam on the lower edge.

Making a smoking cap

When making the cap on pages 72–79, before you begin be sure to plan the size of the circumference. Once the embroidery is completed, block it back to the required size. Trim the unworked canvas around the top of the cap and the edge to about 1.5 cm (½ in).

Choose a lining that matches the background and cut two pieces to the exact sizes of the two blocked and trimmed pieces. With right sides facing, join the needlepoint edge into a ring, hand or machine stitching the seam close to the embroidery stitches at the ends. Press the seam open.

Then with the right sides facing, pin and stitch the edge to the circular top of the cap, again sewing as close to the embroidery as possible. Turn right side out. If any unworked canvas is visible on the right side around the edge of the circle, fill in with tent stitches using the background colour.

Join the lining pieces together as for the canvas pieces and press. Fold the lower edge of the rim to the wrong side on both the lining and the cap, and baste in place. Insert the lining inside the cap and hand stitch the pieces together along the folded edges.

Attach the cord with a tassel to the top of the cap if desired, forming four loops radiating from the centre as shown. When stitching the tassel in place, sew through the lining to secure it to the top of the cap.

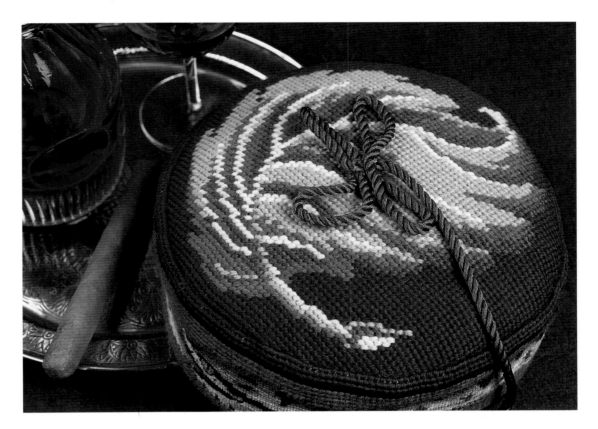

Making a belt

The edge of the Snake Smoking Cap can be used to make a needlepoint belt instead. Before stitching the embroidery for a belt, make sure it will be long enough to fit your waist, overlap by at least 13 cm (5 in), and provide an extra 2.5 cm (1 in) for attaching the buckle. If desired, you can embroider one end of the belt to form a curve or a point.

Block the completed embroidery in the usual way. Then trim the unworked canvas to about 1.5 cm (½ in) around the edge, turn it to the wrong side and baste.

For backing the belt, purchase a piece of firmly woven fabric in a colour that matches the needlepoint background. Cut the backing fabric to the same size as the belt plus 1.5 cm (½ in) extra all around. Turn the extra fabric to the wrong side and press. Hand stitch the backing to the needlepoint using a matching thread. (Note that if you wish to make the belt firmer, you can insert special belt stiffening between the canvas and the lining.)

Choose a buckle without a prong so that the needlepoint will not have to be pierced for eyelet holes. Fold one end of the belt over the bar at the centre of the buckle and stitch in place on the wrong side.

Making a rug

The needlepoint Seashells on pages 88–95 have been designed to be used for individual cushions, or used together for a rug and repeated as many times as desired. To make a needlepoint rug with a repeat pattern such as this, first plan the size of the rug and the positioning of the designs. It is best to work the entire rug on a single piece of canvas, so take this into account when calculating the number of shell repeats.

Wait to purchase the canvas until you have decided on the shell layout. Although the instructions call for a double-thread canvas, you may wish to use an interlock canvas instead since it will provide a stiffer base. If, however, you are considering using the rug as a wall hanging, stick to the softer double-thread canvas.

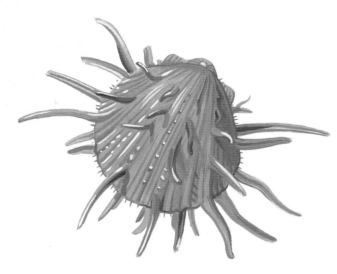

As an aid to positioning the shells, you can count the canvas threads and baste lines around the outline of each of the shell designs before beginning.

After completing the embroidery, block the canvas as usual. Then trim the unworked canvas to 2 cm (¾ in) all around the needlepoint, fold it to the wrong side and baste.

For the backing, choose a strong natural fabric such as hessian (burlap). Cut the backing to the same size as the rug plus a 2 cm (¾ in) turning. Fold the raw edge of the backing to the wrong side and press. Using a strong thread, hand stitch the backing to the needlepoint all around the edge.

CONVERSION CHARTS

Thread amounts and colour numbers are given for each of the projects in the book. It is best to use the recommended brand since colours from substitute brands will not match the originals exactly. If, however, the recommended brand is not available, you may wish to use the alternatives provided on the following pages. Read the information about threads before purchasing any substitutes.

COLOUR NUMBERS

The colour descriptions in the instructions are included as a general guide and are not necessarily the names given by the thread manufacturers. When ordering embroidery threads, always quote the colour numbers rather than the names.

YARN QUANTITIES

Every effort has been made to ensure that the number of skeins given in the instructions will be sufficient. The amount used will vary from stitcher to stitcher. It will also depend on the tent-stitch technique employed; for instance, the half-cross tent stitch technique requires less thread per stitch (see page 116). Because of these discrepencies, the amounts quoted in the instructions are for the tent-stitch techniques that require the most thread per stitch.

PURCHASING AN ALTERNATIVE BRAND

If you are not able to purchase the embroidery thread brand given in the project instructions, you can use the alternative provided below. Because not all brands come in the same size of skein and because in some instances a different number of strands will be required, you should check that the yarn amounts will be sufficient especially for background and border colours before you begin the tapestry.

The skein sizes for the various brands and number of strands to use for different canvas gauges are given below.

Appleton skein and hank sizes

Appleton crewel wool: 25 metres (27 yards) per skein, or 182 metres (200 yards) per hank; use three strands for 10-gauge double thread or 12-gauge single-thread canvas, two strands for 14-gauge, and one strand for 20-gauge *petit point*.
Appleton tapestry wool: 10 metres (11 yards) per skein, or 55 metres (60 yards) per hank; use one strand for 10-gauge double-thread or 12-gauge single-thread canvas.

DMC skein sizes

DMC Médicis: 25 metres (27 yard) per skein; use four strands for 10-gauge double thread or 12-gauge single-thread canvas, three strands for 14-gauge, and two strands for 20-gauge *petit point*.
DMC Laine Colbert: 8 metres (8¼ yards) per skein; use one strand for 10-gauge double-thread or 12-gauge single-thread canvas.
DMC stranded cotton (floss): six 8 metre (9 yard) strands per skein; use 12 strands for 12-gauge double-thread canvas, and two strands for 24-gauge *petit point*.

Anchor skein sizes

Anchor tapestry wool: 10 metres (11 yards) per skein; use one strand for 10-gauge double-thread or 12-gauge single-thread canvas.
Anchor stranded cotton (floss): six 8 metre (9 yard) strands per skein; use 12 strands for 12-gauge double-thread canvas, and two strands for 24-gauge *petit point*.

EMBROIDERY THREAD ALTERNATIVES TABLE

The following alternatives could be used for the various projects. Read the information on page 130 about recalculating yarn amounts before purchasing alternatives.

pages 12–15

Cabbage Cushion

DMC *Laine Colbert* tapestry wool in the following shades could be used as an approximate substitute for this design.

pale blue	7799
light blue	7283
light medium blue	7798
medium blue	7304
dark medium blue	7695
dark blue	7306
deep blue	7307
dark mauve	7375
deep mauve	7372
dark rose	7207
light brown	7413
beige	7511
oatmeal	ecru
pale green	7420

pages 16–19

Insects Glasses Case

Appleton crewel wool in the following shades could be used as an approximate substitute for this design. (Note that one strand of this crewel wool should be used for the *petit point* and three strands for the *gros point*.)

black	993
charcoal	967
dark grey	965
medium grey	964
light grey	962
medium brown	952
dark khaki	345
light khaki	242
sage green	402
light brown	984
gold	843
lemon	552
dark red	504
medium red	501

dark brick	767
medium brick	765
light brick	204
pale pink	751
off-white	991

pages 20–25

Rosa Mundi Cushion

DMC *Laine Colbert* tapestry wool in the following shades could be used as an approximate substitute for this design.

medium sea green	7690
pastel grey blue	7715
pale blue	7828
light blue	7802
white	blanc
medium grey	7618
black	noir
dark grey	7705
dark grey green	7702
off-white	ecru
pale raspberry	7202
light raspberry	7204
medium raspberry	7210
dark raspberry	7138
pastel green	7422
light olive green	7548
medium green	7344
dark green	7385
light gold	7078
medium gold	7505
dark gold	7780
light golden brown	7494
dark golden brown	7488
pale rose pink	7213
medium rose pink	7205
dark rose pink	7961

pages 26–29

Frog Pincushion

DMC stranded cotton (floss) in the following shades could be used as an approximate substitute for this design.

deep blue	336
dark blue	312
medium blue	798
light medium blue	334
light blue	800
pale blue	775
charcoal	413
black	310
off-white	822
straw	3046

pages 30–35

Mouse and Teapot Tea Cosy

DMC *Médicis* crewel wool in the following shades could be used as an approximate substitute for this design. (Note that three strands of this crewel wool should be used for the 14-gauge canvas.)

medium rose pink	8221
light rose pink	8816
dark dusty rose	8125
light dusty rose	8119
chocolate brown	8610
medium golden brown	8321
light golden brown	8322
light camel	8504
pastel pink brown	8842
off-white	ecru
deep khaki brown	8309
dark khaki	8422
medium grey brown	8307
light grey brown	8308
pastel grey brown	8505
white	blanc

page 36–41

Chinese Vases Cushion

DMC *Laine Colbert* tapestry wool in the following shades could be used as an approximate substitute for this design:

yellow	7727
light gold	7504
medium gold	7484
dark gold	7780
lemon	7431
pale blue	7799
light blue	7798
medium blue	7317
dark blue	7319
black	noir
pastel grey	7715
pale grey blue	7568
light grey	7558
pale green blue	7298
white	blanc
pale moss green	7371
light brown	7509
medium brown	7413
dark dusty rose	7840
mid dusty rose	7949
medium brick	7356
dark brick	7167
light dusty rose	7193
pastel pink-grey	7300
light beige pink	7260
medium grey	7620

pages 42–47

Monkey Cushion

DMC *Laine Colbert* tapestry wool in the following shades could be used as an approximate substitute for this design.

white	blanc
pale grey	7715
pale turquoise	7301
light grey green	7404

light yellow 7078
gold 7494
light camel 7739
light nutmeg 7455
mid nutmeg 7508
light sage green 7402
dark sage green 7426
dark khaki 7391
bright green 7344
dark green 7347
off-white ....ecru
pale beige 7450
pale sage green 7400
light beige green 7371
light brown 7413
light grey 7617
medium steel grey 7620
dark grey 7622
charcoal 7538
black ....noir
light terracotta 7164
medium terracotta 7356
medium red 7108
dark red 7110

pages 48–53
Cheetah Footstool

DMC *Laine Colbert* tapestry wool in the following shades could be used as an approximate substitute for this design.

dark red 7110
medium red 7108
cherry 7666
light terracotta 7919
light nutmeg 7445
medium yellow 7484
light yellow 7727
deep brown green 7619
deep brown olive 7391
dark grey green 7426
gold 7474
light camel 7739
pastel camel 7579
off-white ....ecru
dark grey blue 7592
medium blue 7593
light blue 7301
dark grey 7275

medium grey 7273
light grey 7282
pastel blue grey 7715
white ....blanc

page 54–57
Tortoise Doorstop

DMC *Médicis* crewel wool in the following shades could be used as an approximate substitute for this design. (Note that three strands of this crewel wool should be used for the 14-gauge canvas.)

deep brown 8500
deep khaki 8422
khaki green 8412
medium brown olive 8400
pale brown olive 8305
medium olive green 8418
light olive green 8419
light grey green 8420
pale grass green 8871
pale grey green 8421
medium grey 8380
pale grey 8381
off-white ....ecru
dusty rose 8109
medium brown 8307
light brown 8308
medium beige 8505
pale beige 8512
golden brown 8302
medium gold 8325
light gold 8026
lemon 8027

pages 58–63
Begonia Cushion

Anchor tapestry wool in the following shades could be used as an approximate substitute for this design.

dark coral 8240
medium coral 8260
light coral 8306
pale coral 8344
off-white 9382
beige 9654
light brown 9366
medium brown 9368

dark brown green 9068
dark khaki green 9264
medium khaki green 9202
medium grass green 9102
light grass green 9164
light grey green 9172
pale green 9092
pale khaki 9322
pale grey blue 8704
light blue 8784
medium blue 8626

pages 64–68
Bat Evening Bag

Appleton crewel wool in the following shades could be used as an approximate substitute for this design. (Note that one strand of this crewel wool should be used for the *petit point* and three strands for the *gros point*.)

deep brown 586
charcoal 967
dark grey 965
dark blue 325
medium blue 323
light blue 564
pale blue 562
medium grey 962
light grey 989
light brown 902
gold 693
khaki 241
off-white 871
white 991B

pages 68–71
Moon Evening Bag

Appleton crewel wool in the following shades could be used as an approximate substitute for this design. (Note that one strand of this crewel wool should be used for the *petit point* and three strands for the *gros point*.)

dark blue 325
dark grey 965
medium blue 323
light blue 564
pale blue 562
medium grey 962

light grey 989
white 91B
gold 693

pages 72–79
Snake Smoking Cap

DMC *Médicis* crewel wool in the following shades could be used as an approximate substitute for this design. (Note that two strands of this crewel wool should be used for the *petit point* and four strands for the *gros point*.)

Side of cap/belt

burgundy 8123
gold 8302
medium green 8344
black ....noir
charcoal 8713
dark grey 8507
medium grey 8618
light grey 8508
pastel beige grey 8509
bright white ....blanc

Top of cap

burgundy 8123
dark green 8422
medium green 8344
light green 8419
oatmeal 8512

pages 80–87
Pug Cushion

DMC *Médicis* crewel wool in the following shades could be used as an approximate substitute for this design. (Note that two strands of this crewel wool should be used for the *petit point* and four strands for the *gros point*.)

dark scarlet 8103
medium coral 8129
light dusty rose 8119
pale coral 8139
pastel pink beige 8842
pastel grey beige 8502
off-white ....ecru
black ....noir
deep brown 8500
dark brown 8839

golden brown 8610
dark gold 8302
light gold 8313
yellow 8748
mid beige 8504
pastel green 8871
mid grey olive 8412
mid grey green 8406
light grey green 8405
light blue green 8426
light brown 8505
pastel beige green 8381
dark blue 8899
mid blue 8798
light green blue 8214
pastel blue 8211
charcoal 8506
mid brown 8120
mid grey 8618
light grey 8380

pages 88–95
Seashells
DMC *Laine Colbert* tapestry wool in the following shades could be used as an approximate substitute for this design:

Shell 1
dark brown 7477
medium brown 7423
dusty coral 7175
medium gold 7494
light coral 7739
light khaki 7493
light gold 7503
pale brown 7501
beige 7141
pale coral 7746
grape 7255
lilac 7896
light blue 7301
dark grey brown 7275
medium grey 7618
light grey blue 7568
pale grey 7715
off-white ....ecru

Shell 2
medium gold 7494
light gold 7503
beige 7141
dark khaki 7353
mid yellow 7504
light yellow 7078
light blue 7301
dark grey 7626
medium grey 7618
light grey 7282
pale grey 7715
off-white ....ecru

Shell 3
dark rose 7432
medium rose 7840
light rose 7223
pale rose 7120
off-white ....ecru
medium gold 7494
light coral 7739
light gold 7503
beige 7141
medium grey 7618

Shell 4
medium gold 7494
light gold 7503
beige 7141
off-white ....ecru
deep khaki 7391
mid khaki 7512
pale grey-green 7321
medium grey 7618

pages 96–103
Sunflower Chair
Appleton crewel wool in the following shades could be used as an approximate substitute for this design. (Note that three strands of this crewel wool should be used for the 12-gauge canvas. For the mixed background in pastel beige and off-white, use two strands of pastel beige 882 and one strand of off-white 991 together in the needle.)

Chair back
dark gold 695
medium gold 473
medium yellow 471
light yellow 996
pastel yellow 841
deep brown 187
medium brown 185
light brown 301
deep green 646
dark green 644
medium grey green 402
light grass green 235
light grey green 401
pastel grey green 874
pastel beige 882
off-white 991

Chair seat
tan brown 952
cinnamon 764
dark gold 695
medium gold 473
medium yellow 471
pastel yellow 841
pastel beige 882
off-white 991

pages 104–107
Strawberry and Bee Pincushion
DMC *Médicis* crewel wool in the following shades could be used as an approximate substitute for this design. (Note that two strands of this crewel wool should be used for the *petit point* and four strands for the *gros point*.)

dark rose 8106
mid rose 8817
light rose 8223
pale rose 8224
off-white ....ecru
coral 8175
gold 8484
yellow 8748
mid green 8406
light blue green 8426
light green 8419
black ....noir
charcoal 8713
light grey 8618
pale blue grey 8509

pages 108–113
Stone Face Cushion
DMC *Laine Colbert* tapestry wool in the following shades could be used as an approximate substitute for this design.

deep grey brown 7535
deep chocolate brown 7469
medium brick brown 7938
dark chocolate brown 7533
medium nutmeg 7466
dark khaki brown 7490
deep cinnamon 7488
deep grey 7624
dark cinnamon 7514
dark grey 7622
mid chocolate brown 7416
medium khaki 7512
light cinnamon 7524
mid cinnamon 7465
light brown 7415
medium grey 7626
pastel chocolate brown 7519
dark dusty rose 7224
light grey 7620
light nutmeg 7455
pale khaki 7494
pastel pink brown 7461
pastel coral brown 7282
beige 7520
oatmeal 7500
pastel grey green 7270

LIST OF SUPPLIERS

The embroidery threads used in the Graham Rust needlepoints (and suggested as substitutes)
are widely available in large department stores and specialist needlework shops. See below for a stockist near you or
contact the thread companies or the distributors listed here.

APPLETON

United Kingdom

APPLETON BROS LTD,
Thames Works,
Church Street, Chiswick,
London W4 2PE
Tel: (0181) 994 0711
Fax: (0181) 995 6609

North America

ACCESS COMMODITIES
PO Box 1355, Terrell,
Texas 75160
Tel: (972) 563 3313
Wholesale only

THE ELEGANT NEEDLE LTD
7945 MacArthur Boulevard, Suite 203,
Cabin John, Maryland 20818

EWE TWO LTD
24 North Merion Avenue, Bryn Mawr,
Pennsylvania 19010

FLEUR DE PARIS
5835 Washington Boulevard,
Culver City, California 90230

THE JOLLY NEEDLEWOMAN
5810 Kennett Pike,
Centreville, Delaware 19807

THE LACEMAKER
4602 Mahoning Avenue, NW, Suite C,
Warren, Ohio 44483

NEEDLE ARTS STUDIO INC.
115 Metairie Road, Suite B,
Metairie, LA 70005

NEEDLEPOINT INC.
420 Sutter Street, San Francisco,
California 94108

POTPOURRI ETC
209 Richmond Street, El Sigundo,
California 90245

SALLY S. BOOM
Wildwood Studio, PO Box 303,
Montrose, Alabama 36559

SIGN OF THE ARROW
- 1867 FOUNDATION INC.
9740 Clayton Road, St Louis,
Missouri 63124

DICK AND JANE
2352 West 41st Avenue, Vancouver,
British Columbia V6M 2A4

FANCYWORKS
110-3960 Quadra Street, Victoria,
British Columbia V8X 4A3

JET HANDCRAFT STUDIO LTD
PO Box 911103, West Vancouver,
British Columbia V7V 3N3

POINTERS
99 Yorkville Avenue, Unit 103, Toronto,
Ontario M5R 3K5

THREADNEEDLE HOUSE
PO Box 239, Mahone Bay, Nova Scotia,
B0J 2E0

Australia and New Zealand

PENGUIN THREADS PTY
25–27 Izett Street, Prahran,
Victoria, 3181

STADIA HANDCRAFTS
PO Box 357, Beaconsfield, New South
Wales 2014

P.L. STONEWALL & CO PTY LTD
(Flag Division),
52 Erskine Street, Sydney

NANCY'S EMBROIDERY LTD
273 Tinakori Road, PO Box 245,
Thorndon, Wellington

ANCHOR

United Kingdom

COATS PATONS CRAFTS
McMullen Road, Darlington, County
Durham DL1 1YQ
Tel: (01325) 39 43 94
Fax: (01325) 39 42 00

North America

COATS & CLARK
Susan Bates Inc, 30 Patewood Drive,
Greenville, South Carolina 29615
Tel: (800) 243 08 10
Fax: (864) 877 61 17

COATS PATONS CANADA
1001 Roselawn Avenue, Toronto,
Ontario M6B 1B8
Tel: (416) 782 4481
Fax: (416) 785 1370

Australia and New Zealand

COATS PATONS CRAFTS
89–91 Peters Avenue, Mulgrave,
Victoria 3170
Tel: (03) 9561 2288
Fax: (03) 9561 2298

COATS SPENCER CRAFTS
East Tamaki, Auckland
Tel: (09) 274 01 16
Fax: (09) 274 05 84

DMC

Contact the following organisations for
your local stockists:

United Kingdom

DMC CREATIVE WORLD LTD
Pullman Road, Wigston,
Leicestershire LE18 2DY
Tel: (0116) 281 1040
Fax: (0116) 281 3592

North America

DMC CORPORATION
Building 10, Port Kearny, South Kearny,
New Jersey 07032
Tel: (201) 589 0606
Fax: (201) 589 8931

Australia

DMC NEEDLECRAFT PTY LTD
51–66 Carrington Road, Marrickville,
NSW 2204 or
PO Box 317, Earlswood, NSW 2206
Tel: (02) 9559 3088
Fax: (02) 9559 5338

ACKNOWLEDGEMENTS

I would like to thank Rui Paes for his encouragement and advice with the designs for this book and Janet Ravenscroft for her patience and skill, in conjunction with Sally Harding, in editing Needlepoint Designs. Shona Wood's excellent photographs have brought to life all of these images, in Janet James's sympathetic design of the book, for which I am most grateful.

Without the help of Kathleen Mackenzie and Mona Perlhagen of Chelsea Textiles, few of these designs would have materialised, and last but not least I wish to thank Hugh and Debby Illingworth for their painstaking work on the charts.

A number of the designs featured in this book are available as needlepoint kits from:

UNITED KINGDOM
EHRMAN
14–16 Lancer Square
Kensington Church Street
London W8 4EH
Tel: 0171-937 4568
Fax: 0171-937 8552

NORTH AMERICA
EHRMAN TAPESTRY
5300 Dorsey Hall Drive
Suite 110
Ellicott City
MD 21042

Tollfree Order Line: 888 826 8600
Customer service: 410 884 7944
Fax: 410 884 0598
e-mail: usehrman@clark.net